edexcel
advancing learning, changing lives

BTEC National
IT Practitioners

Study Guide

A PEARSON COMPANY

BTEC National Study Guide: IT Practitioners

Published by:
Edexcel Limited
One90 High Holborn
London WC1V 7BH
www.edexcel.org.uk

Distributed by:
Pearson Education Limited
Edinburgh Gate
Harlow
Essex CM20 2JE

First published 2007
Second impression 2008

ISBN 978-1-84690-219-2

Project managed and typeset by Hart McLeod, Cambridge
Printed in Great Britain by Henry Ling Limited, at the Dorset Press, Dorchester, DT1 1HD

Cover image ©Stocksearch/Alamy

The publisher's policy is to use paper manufactured from sustainable forests.

The Publishers and authors are grateful for the following for permission to reproduce copyright materials:
Page 87 Birmingham City Council; Page 117 - text extracted from Peter Honey & Alan Mumford, *The Learning Styles Questionnaire*, 80-item version, Peter Honey Publications, 2006,
ISBN 1-902899-29-6.
Every effort has been made to trace copyright holders and we apologise in advance for any unintentional omissions. We would be pleased to insert the appropriate acknowledgement in any subsequent edition of this publication.

This material offers high quality support for the delivery of Edexcel qualifications.
This does not mean that it is essential to achieve any Edexcel qualification, nor does it mean that this is the only suitable material available to support any Edexcel qualification. No Edexcel-published material will be used verbatim in setting any Edexcel assessment and any resource lists produced by Edexcel shall include this and other appropriate texts.

Contents

PREFACE   4

INTRODUCTION – SEVEN STEPS TO SUCCESS ON YOUR BTEC NATIONAL   5

    Step One – Understand your course and how it works   6

    Step Two – Understand how you are assessed and graded – and use this knowledge to your advantage!   8

    Step Three – Use your time wisely   11

    Step Four – Utilise all your resources   13

    Step Five – Understand your assessment   16

    Step Six – Sharpen your skills   22

    Step Seven – Maximise your opportunities and manage your problems   28

GLOSSARY   32

ACTIVITIES

    UNIT 1 – Communication and Employability Skills for IT   40

    UNIT 2 – Computer Systems   55

    UNIT 3 – Information Systems   77

    UNIT 15 – Organisational Systems Security   93

MARKED ASSIGNMENTS

UNIT 1 – Communication and Employability Skills for IT

    Sample assignment   104

    Pass level answer   106

    Merit level answer   115

    Distinction level answer   129

UNIT 3 – Information Systems

    Sample assignment   135

    Pass level answer   137

    Pass and Merit level answer   139

    Distinction level answer   145

PREFACE

If you've already followed a BTEC First programme, you will know that this is an exciting way to study; if you are fresh from GCSEs you will find that from now on you will be in charge of your own learning. This guide has been written specially for you, to help get you started and then succeed on your BTEC National course.

The **Introduction** concentrates on making sure you have all the right facts about your course at your fingertips. Also, it guides you through the important skills you need to develop if you want to do well including:

- managing your time
- researching information
- preparing a presentation.

Keep this by your side throughout your course and dip into it whenever you need to.

The **Activities** give you tasks to do on your own, in a small group or as a class. They will help you internalise your learning and then prepare for assessment by practising your skills and showing you how much you know. These activities are not for assessment.

The sample **Marked Assignments** show you what other students have done to gain Pass, Merit or Distinction. By seeing what past students have done, you should be able to improve your own grade.

Your BTEC National will cover six, twelve or eighteen units depending on whether you are doing an Award, Certificate or Diploma. In this guide the activities cover sections from Unit 1 – Communication and Employability Skills for IT, Unit 2 – Computer Systems, Unit 3 – Information Systems and Unit 15 – Organisational Systems Security. These units underpin your study of IT (Practitioners).

Because this guide covers only four units, it is essential that you do all the other work your tutors set you. You will have to research information in textbooks, in the library and on the Internet. You should have the opportunity to visit local organisations and welcome visiting speakers to your institution. This is a great way to find out more about your chosen vocational area – the type of jobs that are available and what the work is really like.

This Guide is a taster, an introduction to your BTEC National. Use it as such and make the most of the rich learning environment that your tutors will provide for you. Your BTEC National will give you an excellent base for further study, a broad understanding of IT and the knowledge you need to succeed in the world of work. Remember, thousands of students have achieved a BTEC National and are now studying for a degree or at work, building a successful career.

INTRODUCTION

SEVEN STEPS TO SUCCESS ON YOUR BTEC NATIONAL

You have received this guide because you have decided to do a BTEC National qualification. You may even have started your course. At this stage you should feel good about your decision. BTEC Nationals have many benefits – they are well-known and respected qualifications, they provide excellent preparation for future work or help you to get into university if that is your aim. If you are already at work then gaining a BTEC National will increase your value to your employer and help to prepare you for promotion.

Despite all these benefits though, you may be rather apprehensive about your ability to cope. Or you may be wildly enthusiastic about the whole course! More probably, you are somewhere between the two – perhaps quietly confident most of the time but sometimes worried that you may get out of your depth as the course progresses. You may be certain you made the right choice or still have days when your decision worries you. You may understand exactly what the course entails and what you have to do – or still feel rather bewildered, given all the new stuff you have to get your head around.

Your tutors will use the induction sessions at the start of your course to explain the important information they want you to know. At the time, though, it can be difficult to remember everything. This is especially true if you have just left school and are now studying in a new environment, among a group of people you have only just met. It is often only later that you think of useful questions to ask. Sometimes, misunderstandings or difficulties may only surface weeks or months into a course – and may continue for some time unless they are quickly resolved.

This student guide has been written to help to minimise these difficulties, so that you get the most out of your BTEC National course from day one. You can read through it at your own pace. You can look back at it whenever you have a problem or query.

This Introduction concentrates on making sure you have all the right facts about your course at your fingertips. This includes a **Glossary** (on page 32) which explains the specialist terms you may hear or read – including words and phrases highlighted in bold type in this Introduction.

The Introduction also guides you through the important skills you need to develop if you want to do well – such as managing your time, researching information and preparing a presentation; as well as reminding you about the key skills you will need to do justice to your work, such as good written and verbal communications.

Make sure you have all the right facts

5

- Use the PlusPoints boxes in each section to help you to stay focused on the essentials.

- Use the Action Points boxes to check out things you need to know or do right now.

- Refer to the Glossary (on page 32) if you need to check the meaning of any of the specialist terms you may hear or read.

Remember, thousands of students have achieved BTEC National Diplomas and are now studying for a degree or at work, building a successful career. Many were nervous and unsure of themselves at the outset – and very few experienced absolutely no setbacks during the course. What they did have, though, was a belief in their own ability to do well if they concentrated on getting things right one step at a time. This Introduction enables you to do exactly the same!

STEP ONE

UNDERSTAND YOUR COURSE AND HOW IT WORKS

What is a BTEC qualification and what does it involve? What will you be expected to do on the course? What can you do afterwards? How does this National differ from 'A' levels or a BTEC First qualification?

All these are common questions – but not all prospective students ask them! Did you? And, if so, did you really listen to the answers? And can you remember them now?

If you have already completed a BTEC First course then you may know some of the answers – although you may not appreciate some of the differences between that course and your new one.

Let's start by checking out the basics.

- All BTEC National qualifications are **vocational** or **work-related**. This doesn't mean that they give you all the skills that you need to do a job. It does mean that you gain the specific knowledge and understanding relevant to your chosen subject or area of work. This means that when you start in a job you will learn how to do the work more quickly and should progress further. If you are already employed, it means you become more valuable to your employer. You can choose to study a BTEC National in a wide range of vocational areas, such as Business, Health and Social Care, IT, Performing Arts and many others.

- There are three types of BTEC National qualification and each has a different number of units.

  – The BTEC National Award usually has 6 units and takes 360 **guided learning hours (GLH)** to complete. It is often offered as a part-time or short course but you may be one of the many students doing an Award alongside 'A' levels as a full-time course. An Award is equivalent to one 'A' level.

  – The BTEC National Certificate usually has 12 units and takes 720 GLH to complete. You may be able to study for the Certificate on a part-time or full-time course. It is equivalent to two 'A' levels.

– The BTEC National Diploma usually has 18 units and takes 1080 GLH to complete. It is normally offered as a two-year full-time course. It is equivalent to three 'A' levels.

These qualifications are often described as **nested**. This means that they fit inside each other (rather like Russian dolls!) because the same units are common to them all. This means that if you want to progress from one to another you can do so easily by simply completing more units.

- Every BTEC National qualification has a set number of **core units**. These are the compulsory units every student must complete. The number of core units you will do on your course depends upon the vocational area you are studying.

- All BTEC National qualifications also have a range of **specialist units** from which you may be able to make a choice. These enable you to study particular areas in more depth.

- Some BTEC National qualifications have **specialist core units**. These are mandatory units you will have to complete if you want to follow a particular pathway in certain vocational areas. Engineering is an example of a qualification with the over-arching title, Engineering, which has a set of core units that all students must complete. Then, depending on what type of engineering a student wants to follow, there are more specialist core units that must be studied.

- On all BTEC courses you are expected to be in charge of your own learning. If you have completed a BTEC First, you will already have been introduced to this idea, but you can expect the situation to be rather different now that you are working at BTEC National level. Students on a BTEC First course will be expected to need more guidance whilst they develop their skills and find their feet. In some cases, this might last quite some time. On a BTEC National course you will be expected to take more responsibility for yourself and your own learning, almost from the outset. You will quickly be expected to start thinking for yourself. This means planning what to do and carrying out a task without needing constant reminders. This doesn't mean that your tutor won't give you help and guidance when you need it. It does mean, though, that you need to be 'self-starting' and to be able to use your own initiative. You also need to be able to assess your own performance and make improvements when necessary. If you enjoy having the freedom to make your own decisions and work at your own pace then you will welcome this type of learning with open arms. However, there are dangers! If you are a procrastinator (look up this word if you don't know what it means!) then it's quite likely you will quickly get in a muddle. In this case read Step 3 – Use your time wisely – very carefully indeed!

- The way you are assessed and graded on a BTEC course is different from an 'A' level course, although you will still obtain UCAS points which you need if you want to go to university. You can read about this in the next section.

PLUSPOINTS

+ You can usually choose to study part-time or full-time for your BTEC National and do an Award, Certificate or Diploma, and progress easily from one to the other.

+ You will study both core units and specialist units on your course.

+ When you have completed your BTEC course you can get a job (or **apprenticeship**), use your qualification to develop your career and/or continue your studies to degree level.

+ You are responsible for your own learning on a BTEC course. This prepares you for life at work or at university when you will be expected to be self-starting and to use your own initiative.

ACTION POINTS

✓ Check you know whether you are studying for an Award, Certificate or Diploma and find out the number of units you will be studying for your BTEC National qualification.

✓ Find out which are core and which are specialist units, and which specialist units are offered at your school or college.

✓ Check out the length of your course and when you will be studying each unit.

✓ Explore the Edexcel website at www.edexcel.org.uk. Your first task is to find what's available for your particular BTEC National qualification. Start by finding National qualifications, then look for your vocational area and check you are looking at the 2007 schemes. Then find the specification for your course. Don't print this out – it is far too long. You could, of course, save it if you want to refer to it regularly or you could just look through it for interest and then bookmark the pages relating to your qualification for future reference.

✓ Score yourself out of 5 (where 0 is awful and 5 is excellent) on each of the following to see how much improvement is needed for you to become responsible for your own learning!

Being punctual; organisational ability; tidiness; working accurately; finding and correcting own mistakes; solving problems; accepting responsibility; working with details; planning how to do a job; using own initiative; thinking up new ideas; meeting deadlines.

✓ Draw up your own action plan to improve any areas where you are weak. Talk this through at your next individual **tutorial**.

STEP TWO

UNDERSTAND HOW YOU ARE ASSESSED AND GRADED – AND USE THIS KNOWLEDGE TO YOUR ADVANTAGE!

If you already have a BTEC First qualification, you may think that you don't need to read this section because you assume that BTEC National is simply more of the same. Whilst there are some broad similarities, you will now be working at an entirely different level and the grades you get for your work could be absolutely crucial to your future plans.

Equally, if you have opted for BTEC National rather than 'A' level because you thought you would have less work (or writing) to do then you need to read this section very carefully. Indeed, if you chose your BTEC National because you thought it would guarantee you an easy life, you are likely to get quite a shock when reality hits home!

It is true that, unlike 'A' levels, there are no exams on a BTEC course. However, to do well you need to understand the importance of your assignments, how these are graded and how these convert into unit points and UCAS points. This is the focus of this section.

Your assignments

On a BTEC National course your learning is assessed by means of **assignments** set by your tutors and given to you to complete throughout your course.

■ Your tutors will use a variety of **assessment methods**, such as case

8

studies, projects, presentations and shows, to obtain evidence of your skills and knowledge to date. You may also be given work-based or **time-constrained** assignments – where your performance might be observed and assessed. It will depend very much on the vocational area you are studying (see also page 16).

- Important skills you will need to learn are how to research information (see page 25) and how to use your time effectively, particularly if you have to cope with several assignments at the same time (see page 12). You may also be expected to work co-operatively as a member of a team to complete some parts of your assignments – especially if you are doing a subject like Performing Arts – or to prepare a presentation (see page 26).

- All your assignments are based on **learning outcomes** set by Edexcel. These are listed for each unit in your course specification. You have to meet *all* the learning outcomes to pass the unit.

Your grades

On a BTEC National course, assignments that meet the learning outcomes are graded as Pass, Merit or Distinction.

- The difference between these grades has very little to do with how much you write! Edexcel sets out the **grading criteria** for the different grades in a **grading grid**. This identifies the **higher-level skills** you have to demonstrate to earn a higher grade. You can find out more about this, and read examples of good (and not so good) answers to assignments at Pass, Merit and Distinction level in the Marked Assignments section starting on page 104. You will also find out more about getting the best grade you can in Step 5 – Understand your assessment – on page 16.

- Your grades for all your assignments earn you **unit points**. The number of points you get for each unit is added together and your total score determines your final grade(s) for the qualification – either Pass, Merit or Distinction. You get one final grade if you are taking a BTEC National Award, two if you are taking a BTEC National Certificate and three if you are taking a BTEC National Diploma.

- Your points and overall grade(s) also convert to **UCAS points**, which you will need if you want to apply to study on a degree course. As an example, if you are studying a BTEC National Diploma, and achieve three final Pass grades you will achieve 120 UCAS points. If you achieve three final Distinction grades the number of UCAS points you have earned goes up to 360.

- It is important to note that you start earning both unit and UCAS points from the very first assignment you complete! This means that if you take a long time to settle into your course, or to start working productively, you could easily lose valuable points for quite some time. If you have your heart set on a particular university or degree course then this could limit your choices. Whichever way you look at it, it is silly to squander potentially good grades for an assignment and their equivalent points, just because you didn't really understand what you had to do – which is why this guide has been written to help you!

9

■ If you take a little time to understand how **grade boundaries** work, you can see where you need to concentrate your efforts to get the best final grade possible. Let's give a simple example. Chris and Shaheeda both want to go to university and have worked hard on their BTEC National Diploma course. Chris ends with a total score of 226 unit points which converts to 280 UCAS points. Shaheeda ends with a total score of 228 unit points – just two points more – which converts to 320 UCAS points! This is because a score of between 204 and 227 unit points gives 280 UCAS points, whereas a score of 228 – 251 points gives 320 UCAS points. Shaheeda is pleased because this increases her chances of getting a place on the degree course she wants. Chris is annoyed. He says if he had known then he would have put more effort into his last assignment to get two points more.

■ It is always tempting to spend time on work you like doing, rather than work you don't – but this can be a mistake if you have already done the best you can at an assignment and it would already earn a very good grade. Instead, you should now concentrate on improving an assignment which covers an area where you know you are weak, because this will boost your overall grade(s). You will learn more about this in Step 3 – Use your time wisely.

PLUSPOINTS

+ Your learning is assessed in a variety of ways, such as by assignments, projects and case studies. You will need to be able to research effectively, manage your own time and work well with other people to succeed.

+ You need to demonstrate specific knowledge and skills to achieve the learning outcomes set by Edexcel. You need to demonstrate you can meet all the learning outcomes to pass a unit.

+ Higher-level skills are required for higher grades. The grading criteria for Pass, Merit and Distinction grades are set out in a grading grid for the unit.

+ The assessment grades of Pass, Merit and Distinction convert to unit points. The total number of unit points you receive during the course determines your final overall grade(s) and the UCAS points you have earned.

+ Working effectively from the beginning maximises your chances of achieving a good qualification grade. Understanding grade boundaries enables you to get the best final grade(s) possible.

ACTION POINTS

✓ Find the learning outcomes for the units you are currently studying. Your tutor may have given you these already, or you can find them in the specification for your course that you already accessed at www.edexcel.org.uk.

✓ Look at the grading grid for the units and identify the way the evidence required changes to achieve the higher grades. Don't worry if there are some words that you do not understand – these are explained in more detail on page 32 of this guide.

✓ If you are still unsure how the unit points system works, ask your tutor to explain it to you.

✓ Check out the number of UCAS points you would need for any course or university in which you are interested.

✓ Keep a record of the unit points you earn throughout your course and check regularly how this is affecting your overall grade(s), based on the grade boundaries for your qualification. Your tutor will give you this information or you can check it yourself in the specification for your course on the Edexcel website.

STEP THREE

USE YOUR TIME WISELY

Most students on a BTEC National course are trying to combine their course commitments with a number of others – such as a job (either full- or part-time) and family responsibilities. In addition, they still want time to meet with friends, enjoy a social life and keep up hobbies and interests that they have.

Starting the course doesn't mean that you have to hide away for months if you want to do well. It does mean that you have to use your time wisely if you want to do well, stay sane and keep a balance in your life.

You will only do this if you make time work for you, rather than against you, by taking control. This means that you decide what you are doing, when you are doing it and work purposefully; rather than simply reacting to problems or panicking madly because you've yet another deadline staring you in the face.

This becomes even more important as your course progresses, because your workload is likely to increase, particularly towards the end of a term. In the early days you may be beautifully organised and able to cope easily. Then you may find you have several tasks to complete simultaneously as well as some research to start. Then you get two assignments in the same week from different tutors – as well as having a presentation to prepare. Then another assignment is scheduled for the following week – and so on. This is not because your tutors are being deliberately difficult. Indeed, most will try to schedule your assignments to avoid such clashes. The problem, of course, is that none of your tutors can assess your abilities until you have learned something – so if several units start and end at the same time it is highly likely there will be some overlap between your assignments.

To cope when the going gets tough, without collapsing into an exhausted heap, you need to learn a few time-management skills.

- **Pinpoint where your time goes at the moment** Time is like money – it's usually difficult to work out where it all went! Work out how much time you currently spend at college, at work, at home and on social activities. Check, too, how much time you waste each week – and why this happens. Are you disorganised or do you easily get distracted? Then identify commitments that are vital and those that are optional, so that you know where you can find time if you need to.

- **Plan when and where to work** It is realistic to expect to do quite a lot of work for your course in your own time. It is also better to work regularly, and in relatively short bursts, than to work just once or twice a week for very long stretches. In addition to deciding when to work, and for how long, you also need to think about when and where to work. If you are a lark, you will work better early in the day; if you are an owl, you will be at your best later on. Whatever time you work, you need somewhere quiet so that you can concentrate and with space for books and other resources you need. If the words 'quiet oasis' and 'your house' are totally incompatible at any time of the day or night then

Use your time wisely

11

check out the opening hours of your local and college library so that you have an escape route if you need it. If you are trying to combine studying with parental responsibilities it is sensible to factor in your children's commitments – and work around their bedtimes too! Store up favours, too, from friends and grandparents that you can call-in if you get desperate for extra time when an assignment deadline is looming.

- **Schedule your commitments** Keep a diary or (even better) a wall chart and write down every appointment you make or task you are given. It is useful to use a colour code to differentiate between personal and work or course commitments. You may also want to enter assignment review dates with your tutor in one colour and final deadline dates in another. Keep your diary or chart up-to-date by adding any new dates promptly every time you receive another task or assignment or whenever you make any other arrangements. Keep checking ahead so that you always have prior warning when important dates are looming. This stops you from planning a heavy social week when you will be at your busiest at work or college and from arranging a dental appointment on the morning when you and your team are scheduled to give an important presentation!

- **Prioritise your work** This means doing the most important and urgent task first, rather than the one you like the most! Normally this will be the task or assignment with the nearest deadline. There are two exceptions. Sometimes you may need to send off for information and allow time for it to arrive. It is therefore sensible to do this first so that you are not held up later. The second is when you have to take account of other people's schedules – because you are working in a team or are arranging to interview someone, for example. In this case you will have to arrange your schedule around their needs, not just your own.

- **Set sensible timescales** Trying to do work at the last minute or in a rush is never satisfactory, so it is wise always to allocate more time than you think you will need, never less. Remember, too, to include all the stages of a complex task or assignment, such as researching the information, deciding what to use, creating a first draft, checking it and making improvements and printing it out. If you are planning to do any of your work in a central facility always allow extra time and try to start work early. If you arrive at the last minute you may find every computer and printer is fully utilised until closing time.

- **Learn self-discipline!** This means not putting things off (procrastinating!) because you don't know where to start or don't feel in the mood. Unless you are ill, you have to find some way of persuading yourself to work. One way is to bribe yourself. Make a start and promise yourself that if you work productively for 30 minutes then you deserve a small reward. After 30 minutes you may have become more engrossed and want to keep going a little longer. At least you have made a start, so it's easier to come back and do more later. It doesn't matter whether you have research to do, an assignment to write up, a coaching session to plan, or lines to learn, you need to be self-disciplined.

- **Take regular breaks and keep your life in balance** Don't go to the opposite extreme and work for hours on end. Take regular breaks to give yourself a rest and a change of activity. You need to recharge your batteries! Similarly, don't cancel every social arrangement so that you can work 24/7. Whilst this may be occasionally necessary if you have several deadlines looming simultaneously, it should only be a last resort. If you find yourself doing this regularly then go back to the beginning of this section and see where your time-management planning is going wrong.

PLUSPOINTS

+ Being in control of your time enables you to balance your commitments according to their importance and allows you not let to anyone down – including yourself.

+ Controlling time involves knowing how you spend (and waste!) your time now, planning when best to do work, scheduling your commitments and setting sensible timescales for work to be done.

+ Knowing how to prioritise means that you will schedule work effectively according to its urgency and importance, but this also requires self-discipline. You have to follow the schedule you have set for yourself!

+ Managing time and focusing on the task at hand means you will do better work and be less stressed, because you are not having to react to problems or crises. You can also find the time to include regular breaks and leisure activities in your schedule.

ACTION POINTS

✓ Find out how many assignments you can expect to receive this term and when you can expect to receive these. Enter this information into your student diary or onto a planner you can refer to regularly.

✓ Update your diary and/or planner with other commitments that you have this term – both work/college-related and social. Identify any potential clashes and decide the best action to take to solve the problem.

✓ Identify your own best time and place to work quietly and effectively.

✓ Displacement activities are things we do to put off starting a job we don't want to do – such as sending texts, watching TV, checking emails etc. Identify yours so that you know when you're doing them!

STEP FOUR

UTILISE ALL YOUR RESOURCES

Your resources are all the things that can help you to achieve your qualification. They can therefore be as wide-ranging as your favourite website and your **study buddy** (see page 15) who collects handouts for you if you miss a class.

Your college will provide the essential resources for your course, such as a library with a wide range of books and electronic reference sources, learning resource centre(s), the computer network and Internet access. Other basic resources you will be expected to provide yourself, such as file folders and paper. The policy on textbooks varies from one college to another, but on most courses, today, students are expected to buy their own. If you look after yours carefully, then you have the option to sell it on to someone else afterwards and recoup some of your money. If you scribble all over it, leave it on the floor and then tread on it, turn back pages and rapidly turn it into a dog-eared, misshapen version of its former self then you miss out on this opportunity.

13

Unfortunately, students often squander other opportunities to utilise resources in the best way – usually because they don't think about them very much, if at all. To help, below is a list of the resources you should consider important – with a few tips on how to get the best out of them.

- **Course information** This includes your course specification, this Study Guide and all the other information relating to your BTEC National which you can find on the Edexcel website. Add to this all the information given to you at college relating to your course, including term dates, assignment dates and, of course, your timetable. This should not be 'dead' information that you glance at once and then discard or ignore. Rather, it is important reference material that you need to store somewhere obvious, so that you can look at it whenever you have a query or need to clarify something quickly.

- **Course materials** In this group is your textbook (if there is one), the handouts you are given as well as print-outs and notes you make yourself. File handouts the moment you are given them and put them into an A4 folder bought for the purpose. You will need one for each unit you study. Some students prefer lever-arch files but these are more bulky so more difficult to carry around all day. Unless you have a locker at college it can be easier to keep a lever-arch file at home for permanent storage of past handouts and notes for a unit and carry an A4 folder with you which contains current topic information. Filing handouts and print-outs promptly means they don't get lost. They are also less likely to get crumpled, torn or tatty, becoming virtually unreadable. Unless you have a private and extensive source of income then this is even more important if you have to pay for every print-out you take in your college resource centre. If you are following a course such as Art and Design, then there will be all your art materials and the pieces you produce. You must look after these with great care.

- **Other stationery items** Having your own pens, pencils, notepad, punch, stapler and sets of dividers is essential. Nothing irritates tutors more than watching one punch circulate around a group – except, perhaps, the student who trudges into class with nothing to write on or with. Your dividers should be clearly labelled to help you store and find notes, print-outs and handouts fast. Similarly, your notes should be clearly headed and dated. If you are writing up notes from your own research then you will have to include your source. Researching information is explained in Step 6 – Sharpen your skills.

- **Equipment and facilities** These include your college library and resource centres, the college computer network and other college equipment you can use, such as laptop computers, photocopiers and presentation equipment. Much of this may be freely available; others – such as using the photocopier in the college library or the printers in a resource centre – may cost you money. Many useful resources will be electronic, such as DVDs or electronic journals and databases. At home you may have your own computer with Internet access to count as a resource. Finally, include any specialist equipment and facilities available for your particular course that you use at college or have at home.

Utilise all your resources

14

All centralised college resources and facilities are invaluable if you know how to use them – but can be baffling when you don't. Your induction should have included how to use the library, resource centre(s) and computer network. You should also have been informed of the policy on using IT equipment, which determines what you can and can't do when you are using college computers. If, by any chance, you missed this then go and check it out for yourself. Library and resource-centre staff will be only too pleased to give you helpful advice – especially if you pick a quiet time to call in. You can also find out about the allowable ways to transfer data between your college computer and your home computer if your options are limited because of IT security.

Having a study buddy is a good idea

- **People** You are surrounded by people who are valuable resources: your tutor(s), specialist staff at college, your employer and work colleagues, your relatives and any friends who have particular skills or who work in the same area you are studying. Other members of your class are also useful resources – although they may not always seem like it! Use them, for example, to discuss topics out of class time. A good debate between a group of students can often raise and clarify issues that there may not be time to discuss fully in class. Having a study buddy is another good idea – you get/make notes for them when they are away and vice versa. That way you don't miss anything.

  If you want information or help from someone, especially anyone outside your immediate circle, then remember to get the basics right! Approach them courteously, do your homework first so that you are well-prepared and remember that you are asking for assistance – not trying to get them to do the work for you! If someone has agreed to allow you to interview them as part of your research for an assignment or project then good preparations will be vital, as you will see in Step 6 – Sharpen your skills (see page 22).

  One word of warning: be wary about using information from friends or relatives who have done a similar or earlier course. First, the slant of the material they were given may be different. It may also be out-of-date. And *never* copy anyone else's written assignments. This is **plagiarism** – a deadly sin in the educational world. You can read more about this in Step 5 – Understand your assessment (see page 16).

- **You!** You have the ability to be your own best resource or your own worst enemy! The difference depends upon your work skills, your personal skills and your attitude to your course and other people. You have already seen how to use time wisely. Throughout this guide you will find out how to sharpen and improve other work and personal skills and how to get the most out of your course – but it is up to you to read it and apply your new-found knowledge! This is why attributes like a positive attitude, an enquiring mind and the ability to focus on what is important all have a major impact on your final result.

PLUSPOINTS

+ Resources help you to achieve your qualification. You will squander these unwittingly if you don't know what they are or how to use them properly.

+ Course information needs to be stored safely for future reference: course materials need to be filed promptly and accurately so that you can find them quickly.

+ You need your own set of key stationery items; you also need to know how to use any central facilities or resources such as the library, learning resource centres and your computer network.

+ People are often a key resource – school or college staff, work colleagues, members of your class, people who are experts in their field.

+ You can be your own best resource! Develop the skills you need to be able to work quickly and accurately and to get the most out of other people who can help you.

ACTION POINTS

✓ Under the same headings as in this section, list all the resources you need for your course and tick off those you currently have. Then decide how and when you can obtain anything vital that you lack.

✓ Check that you know how to access and use all the shared resources to which you have access at school or college.

✓ Pair up with someone on your course as a study buddy – and don't let them down!

✓ Test your own storage systems. How fast can you find notes or print-outs you made yesterday/last week/last month – and what condition are they in?

✓ Find out the IT policy at your school or college and make sure you abide by it.

16

STEP FIVE

UNDERSTAND YOUR ASSESSMENT

The key to doing really, really well on any BTEC National course is to understand exactly what you are expected to do in your assignments – and then to do it! It really is as simple as that. So why is it that some people go wrong?

Obviously, you may worry that an assignment may be so difficult that it is beyond you. Actually this is highly unlikely to happen, because all your assignments are based on topics you will have already covered thoroughly in class. Therefore, if you have attended regularly – and have clarified any queries or worries you have either in class or during your tutorials – this shouldn't happen. If you have had an unavoidably lengthy absence then you may need to review your progress with your tutor and decide how best to cope with the situation. Otherwise, you should note that the main problems with assignments are usually due to far more mundane pitfalls – such as:

✗ not reading the instructions or the assignment brief properly

✗ not understanding what you are supposed to do

✗ only doing part of the task or answering part of a question

✗ skimping the preparation, the research or the whole thing

✗ not communicating your ideas clearly

✗ guessing answers rather than researching properly

✗ padding out answers with irrelevant information

✗ leaving the work until the last minute and then doing it in a rush

✗ ignoring advice and feedback your tutor has given you.

You can avoid all of these traps by following the guidelines below so that you know exactly what you are doing, prepare well and produce your best work.

The assignment 'brief'

The word 'brief' is just another way of saying 'instructions'. Often, though, a 'brief' (despite its name!) may be rather lengthy. The brief sets the context for the work, defines what evidence you will need to produce and matches the grading criteria to the tasks. It will also give you a schedule for completing the tasks. For example, a brief may include details of a case study you have to read; research you have to carry out or a task you have to do, as well as questions you have to answer. Or it may give you details about a project or group presentation you have to prepare. The type of assignments you receive will depend partly upon the vocational area you are studying, but you can expect some to be in the form of written assignments. Others are likely to be more practical or project-based, especially if you are doing a very practical subject such as Art and Design, Performing Arts or Sport. You may also be assessed in the workplace. For example, this is a course requirement if you are studying Children's Care, Learning and Development.

The assignment brief may also include the **learning outcomes** to which it relates. These tell you the purpose of the assessment and the knowledge you need to demonstrate to obtain a required grade. If your brief doesn't list the learning outcomes, then you should check this information against the unit specification to see the exact knowledge you need to demonstrate.

The grade(s) you can obtain will also be stated on the assignment brief. Sometimes an assignment will focus on just one grade. Others may give you the opportunity to develop or extend your work to progress to a higher grade. This is often dependent upon submitting acceptable work at the previous grade first. You will see examples of this in the Marked Assignment section of this Study Guide on page 104.

The brief will also tell you if you have to do part of the work as a member of a group. In this case, you must identify your own contribution. You may also be expected to take part in a **peer review**, where you all give feedback on the contribution of one another. Remember that you should do this as objectively and professionally as possible – not just praise everyone madly in the hope that they will do the same for you! In any assignment where there is a group contribution, there is virtually always an individual component, so that your individual grade can be assessed accurately.

Finally, your assignment brief should state the final deadline for handing in the work as well as any interim review dates when you can discuss your progress and ideas with your tutor. These are very important dates indeed and should be entered immediately into your diary or planner. You should schedule your work around these dates so that you have made a start by the first date. This will then enable you to note any queries or significant issues you want to discuss. Otherwise you will waste a valuable opportunity to obtain useful feedback on your progress. Remember, too, to take a notebook to any review meetings so that you can write down the guidance you are given.

Your school or college rules and regulations

Your school or college will have a number of policies and guidelines about assignments and assessment. These will deal with issues such as:

- The procedure you must follow if you have a serious personal problem so cannot meet the deadline date and need an extension.
- Any penalties for missing a deadline date without any good reason.
- The penalties for copying someone else's work (**plagiarism**). These will be severe so make sure that you never share your work (including your CDs) with anyone else and don't ask to borrow theirs.
- The procedure to follow if you are unhappy with the final grade you receive.

Even though it is unlikely that you will ever need to use any of these policies, it is sensible to know they exist, and what they say, just as a safeguard.

Understanding the question or task

There are two aspects to a question or task that need attention. The first are the *command words*, which are explained below. The second are the *presentation instructions*, so that if you are asked to produce a table or graph or report then you do exactly that – and don't write a list or an essay instead!

Command words are used to specify how a question must be answered, eg 'explain', 'describe', 'analyse', 'evaluate'. These words relate to the type of answer required. So whereas you may be asked to 'describe' something at Pass level, you will need to do more (such as 'analyse' or 'evaluate') to achieve Merit or Distinction grade.

Many students fail to get a higher grade because they do not realise the difference between these words. They simply don't know *how* to analyse or evaluate, so give an explanation instead. Just adding to a list or giving a few more details will never give you a higher grade – instead you need to change your whole approach to the answer.

The **grading grid** for each unit of your course gives you the command words, so that you can find out exactly what you have to do in each unit, to obtain a Pass, Merit and Distinction. The following charts show you what is usually required when you see a particular command word. You can use this, and the marked assignments on pages 104–150, to see the difference between the types of answers required for each grade. (The assignments your centre gives you will be specially written to ensure you have the opportunity to achieve all the possible grades.) Remember, though, that these are just examples to guide you. The exact response will often depend upon the way a question is worded, so if you have any doubts at all check with your tutor before you start work.

There are two other important points to note:

- Sometimes the same command word may be repeated for different grades – such as 'create' or 'explain'. In this case the *complexity* or *range* of the task itself increases at the higher grades – as you will see if you read the grading grid for the unit.

- Command words can also vary depending upon your vocational area. If you are studying Performing Arts or Art and Design you will probably find several command words that an Engineer or IT Practitioner would not – and vice versa!

To obtain a Pass grade

To achieve this grade you must usually demonstrate that you understand the important facts relating to a topic and can state these clearly and concisely.

Command word	What this means
Create (or produce)	Make, invent or construct an item.
Describe	Give a clear, straightforward description that includes all the main points and links these together logically.
Define	Clearly explain what a particular term means and give an example, if appropriate, to show what you mean.
Explain . . . how/why	Set out in detail the meaning of something, with reasons. It is often helpful to give an example of what you mean. Start with the topic then give the 'how' or 'why'.
Identify	Distinguish and state the main features or basic facts relating to a topic.
Interpret	Define or explain the meaning of something.
Illustrate	Give examples to show what you mean.
List	Provide the information required in a list rather than in continuous writing.
Outline	Write a clear description that includes all the main points but avoid going into too much detail.
Plan (or devise)	Work out and explain how you would carry out a task or activity.
Select (and present) information	Identify relevant information to support the argument you are making and communicate this in an appropriate way.
State	Write a clear and full account.
Undertake	Carry out a specific activity.
Examples: **Identify** the main features on a digital camera. **Describe** your usual lifestyle. **Outline** the steps to take to carry out research for an assignment.	

19

To obtain a Merit grade

To obtain this grade you must prove that you can apply your knowledge in a specific way.

Command word	What this means
Analyse	Identify separate factors, say how they are related and how each one relates to the topic.
Classify	Sort your information into appropriate categories before presenting or explaining it.
Compare and contrast	Identify the main factors that apply in two or more situations and explain the similarities and differences or advantages and disadvantages.
Demonstrate	Provide several relevant examples or appropriate evidence which support the arguments you are making. In some vocational areas this may also mean giving a practical performance.
Discuss	Provide a thoughtful and logical argument to support the case you are making.
Explain (in detail)	Provide details and give reasons and/or evidence to clearly support the argument you are making.
Implement	Put into practice or operation. You may also have to interpret or justify the effect or result.
Interpret	Understand and explain an effect or result.
Justify	Give appropriate reasons to support your opinion or views and show how you arrived at these conclusions.
Relate/report	Give a full account of, with reasons.
Research	Carry out a full investigation.
Specify	Provide full details and descriptions of selected items or activities.

Examples:
Compare and contrast the performance of two different digital cameras.
Justify your usual lifestyle.
Explain (in detail) the steps to take to research an assignment.

To obtain a Distinction grade

To obtain this grade you must prove that you can make a reasoned judgement based on appropriate evidence.

Command word	What this means
Analyse	Identify the key factors, show how they are linked and explain the importance and relevance of each.
Assess	Give careful consideration to all the factors or events that apply and identify which are the most important and relevant, with reasons for your views.
Comprehensively explain	Give a very detailed explanation that covers all the relevant points and give reasons for your views or actions.
Comment critically	Give your view after you have considered all the evidence, particularly the importance of both the relevant positive and negative aspects.
Evaluate	Review the information and then bring it together to form a conclusion. Give evidence to support each of your views or statements.
Evaluate critically	Review the information to decide the degree to which something is true, important or valuable. Then assess possible alternatives taking into account their strengths and weaknesses if they were applied instead. Then give a precise and detailed account to explain your opinion.
Summarise	Identify and review the main, relevant factors and/or arguments so that these are explained in a clear and concise manner.

Examples:

Assess ten features commonly found on a digital camera.
Evaluate critically your usual lifestyle.
Analyse your own ability to carry out effective research for an assignment.

Responding positively

This is often the most important attribute of all! If you believe that assignments give you the opportunity to demonstrate what you know and how you can apply it *and* positively respond to the challenge by being determined to give it your best shot, then you will do far better than someone who is defeated before they start.

It obviously helps, too, if you are well organised and have confidence in your own abilities – which is what the next section is all about!

PLUSPOINTS

+ Many mistakes in assignments are through errors that can easily be avoided, such as not reading the instructions properly or doing only part of the task that was set!

+ Always read the assignment brief very carefully indeed. Check that you understand exactly what you have to do and the learning outcomes you must demonstrate.

+ Make a note of the deadline for an assignment and any interim review dates on your planner. Schedule work around these dates so that you can make the most of reviews with your tutor.

+ Make sure you know about school or college policies relating to assessment, such as how to obtain an extension or query a final grade.

+ For every assignment, make sure you understand the command words, which tell you how to answer the question, and the presentation instructions, which say what you must produce.

+ Command words are shown in the grading grid for each unit of your qualification. Expect command words and/or the complexity of a task to be different at higher grades, because you have to demonstrate higher-level skills.

ACTION POINTS

✓ Discuss with your tutor the format (style) of assignments you are likely to receive on your course, eg assignments, projects, or practical work where you are observed.

✓ Check the format of the assignments in the Marked Assignments section of this book. Look at the type of work students did to gain a Pass and then look at the difference in the Merit answers. Read the tutor's comments carefully and ask your own tutor if there is anything you do not understand.

✓ Check out all the policies and guidelines at your school or college that relate to assessment and make sure you understand them.

✓ Check out the grading grid for the units you are currently studying and identify the command words for each grade. Then check you understand what they mean using the explanations above. If there are any words that are not included, ask your tutor to explain the meanings and what you would be required to do.

22

STEP SIX

SHARPEN YOUR SKILLS

To do your best in any assignment you need a number of skills. Some of these may be vocationally specific, or professional, skills that you are learning as part of your course – such as acting or dancing if you are taking a Performing Arts course or, perhaps, football if you are following a Sports course. Others, though, are broader skills that will help you to do well in assignments no matter what subjects or topics you are studying – such as communicating clearly and co-operating with others.

Some of these skills you will have already and in some areas you may be extremely proficient. Knowing where your weaknesses lie, though, and doing something about them has many benefits. You will work more quickly, more accurately *and* have increased confidence in your own abilities. As an extra bonus, all these skills also make you more effective at work – so there really is no excuse for not giving yourself a quick skills check and then remedying any problem areas.

This section contains hints and tips to help you check out and improve each of the following areas:

- Your numeracy skills
- Keyboarding and document preparation
- Your IT skills
- Your written communication skills
- Working with others
- Researching information
- Making a presentation

Your numeracy skills

Some people have the idea that they can ignore numeracy because this skill isn't relevant to their vocational area – such as Art and Design or Children's Care, Learning and Development. If this is how you think then you are wrong! Numeracy is a life skill that everyone needs, so if you can't carry out basic calculations accurately then you will have problems, often when you least expect them.

Fortunately there are several things you can do to remedy this situation:

- Practise basic calculations in your head and then check them on a calculator.
- Ask your tutor if there are any essential calculations which give you difficulties.
- Use your onscreen calculator (or a spreadsheet package) to do calculations for you when you are using your computer.
- Try your hand at Sudoku puzzles – either on paper or by using a software package or online at sites such as www.websudoku.com/.
- Investigate puzzle sites and brain-training software, such as http://school.discovery.com/brainboosters/ and Dr Kawashima's Brain Training by Nintendo.
- Check out online sites such as www.bbc.co.uk/skillswise/ and www.bbc.co.uk/schools/ks3bitesize/maths/number/index.shtml to improve your skills.

Numeracy is a life skill

Keyboarding and document preparation

- Think seriously about learning to touch-type to save hours of time! Your school or college may have a workshop you can join or you can learn online such as by downloading a free program at www.sense-lang.org/typing/ or practising on sites such as www.computerlab.kids.new.net/keyboarding.htm.
- Obtain correct examples of document formats you will have to use, such as a report or summary. Your tutor may provide you with these or you can find examples in many communication textbooks.
- Proof-read work you produce on a computer *carefully*. Remember that your spell checker will not pick up every mistake you make, such as a mistyped word that makes another word (eg form/from; sheer/shear)

and grammar checkers, too, are not without their problems! This means you still have to read your work through yourself. If possible, let your work go 'cold' before you do this so that you read it afresh and don't make assumptions about what you have written. Then read word-by-word to make sure it still makes sense and there are no silly mistakes, such as missing or duplicated words.

- Make sure your work looks professional by using an appropriate typeface and font size as well as suitable margins.
- Print-out your work carefully and store it neatly, so it looks in pristine condition when you hand it in.

Your IT skills

- Check that you can use the main features of all the software packages that you will need to produce your assignments, such as Word, Excel and PowerPoint.
- Adopt a good search engine, such as Google, and learn to use it properly. Many have online tutorials such as www.googleguide.com.
- Develop your IT skills to enable you to enhance your assignments appropriately. For example, this may include learning how to import and export text and artwork from one package to another; taking digital photographs and inserting them into your work and/or creating drawings or diagrams by using appropriate software for your course.

Your written communication skills

A poor vocabulary will reduce your ability to explain yourself clearly; work peppered with spelling or punctuation errors looks unprofessional.

- Read more. This introduces you to new words and familiarises you over and over again with the correct way to spell words.
- Look up words you don't understand in a dictionary and then try to use them yourself in conversation.
- Use the Thesaurus in Word to find alternatives to words you find yourself regularly repeating, to add variety to your work.
- *Never* use words you don't understand in the hope that they sound impressive!
- Do crosswords to improve your word power and spelling.
- Resolve to master punctuation – especially apostrophes – either by using an online programme or working your way through the relevant section of a communication textbook that you like.
- Check out online sites such as www.bbc.co.uk/skillswise/ and www.bbc.co.uk/schools/gcsebitesize/english/ as well as puzzle sites with communication questions such as http://school.discovery.com/brainboosters/.

Working with others

In your private life you can choose who you want to be with and how you respond to them. At work you cannot do that – you are paid to be professional and this means working alongside a wide variety of people, some of whom you may like and some of whom you may not!

The same applies at school or college. By the time you have reached BTEC National level you will be expected to have outgrown wanting to work with your best friends on every project! You may not be very keen on everyone who is in the same team as you, but – at the very least – you can be pleasant, co-operative and helpful. In a large group this isn't normally too difficult. You may find it much harder if you have to partner someone who has very different ideas and ways of working to you.

In this case it may help if you:

- Realise that everyone is different and that your ways of working may not always be the best!
- Are prepared to listen and contribute to a discussion (positively) in equal amounts. Make sure, too, that you encourage the quiet members of the group to speak-up, by asking them what their views are. The ability to draw other people into the discussion is an important and valuable skill to learn.
- Write down what you have said you will do, so that you don't forget anything.
- Are prepared to do your fair share of the work.
- Discuss options and alternatives with people – don't give them orders or meekly accept instructions and then resent it afterwards.
- Don't expect other people to do what you wouldn't be prepared to do.
- Are sensitive to other people's feelings and remember that they may have personal problems or issues that affect their behaviour.
- *Always* keep your promises and never let anyone down when they are depending upon you.
- Don't flounce around or lose your temper if things get tough. Instead, take a break while you cool down. Then sit down and discuss the issues that are annoying you.
- Help other people to reach a compromise when necessary, by acting as peacemaker.

Researching information

Poor researchers either cannot find what they want or find too much – and then drown in a pile of papers. If you find yourself drifting aimlessly around a library when you want information or printing out dozens of pages for no apparent purpose, then this section is for you!

- Always check *exactly* what it is you need to find and how much detail is needed. Write down a few key words to keep yourself focused.
- Discipline yourself to ignore anything that is irrelevant – from books with interesting titles to websites which sound tempting but have little to do with your topic or key words.
- Remember that you could theoretically research information forever! So at some time you have to call a halt. Learning when to do this is another skill, but you can learn this by writing out a schedule which clearly states when you have to stop looking and start sorting out your information and writing about it!

- In a library, check you know how the books are stored and what other types of media are available. If you can't find what you are looking for, then ask the librarian for help. Checking the index in a book is the quickest way to find out whether it contains information related to your key words. Put it back if it doesn't or if you can't understand it. If you find three or four books and/or journals that contain what you need then that is usually enough.

- Online, use a good search engine and use the summary of the search results to check out the best sites. Force yourself to check out sites beyond page one of the search results! When you enter a site investigate it carefully – use the site map if necessary. It isn't always easy to find exactly what you want. Bookmark sites you find helpful and will want to use again and only take print-outs when the information is closely related to your key words.

- Talk to people who can help you (see also Step 4 – Utilise all your resources) and prepare in advance by thinking about the best questions to ask. Always explain why you want the information and don't expect anyone to tell you anything that is confidential or sensitive – such as personal information or financial details. Always write clear notes so that you remember what you have been told, by whom and when. If you are wise you will also note down their contact details so that you can contact them again if you think of anything later. If you remember to be courteous and thank them for their help, this shouldn't be a problem.

- Store all your precious information carefully and neatly in a labelled folder so that you can find it easily. Then, when you are ready to start work, reread it and extract that which is most closely related to your key words and the task you are doing.

- Make sure you state the source of all the information you quote by including the name of the author or the web address, either in the text or as part of a bibliography at the end. Your school or college will have a help sheet which will tell you exactly how to do this.

Making a presentation

This involves several skills – which is why it is such a popular way of finding out what students can do! It will test your ability to work in a team, speak in public and use IT (normally PowerPoint) – as well as your nerves. It is therefore excellent practice for many of the tasks you will have to do when you are at work – from attending an interview to talking to an important client.

You will be less nervous if you have prepared well and have rehearsed your role beforehand. You will produce a better, more professional presentation if you take note of the following points.

- If you are working as a team, work out everyone's strengths and weaknesses and divide up the work (fairly) taking these into account. Work out, too, how long each person should speak and who would be the best as the 'leader' who introduces each person and then summarises everything at the end.

PLUSPOINTS

+ Poor numeracy skills can let you down in your assignments and at work. Work at improving these if you regularly struggle with even simple calculations.

+ Good keyboarding, document production and IT skills can save you hours of time and mean that your work is of a far more professional standard. Improve any of these areas which are letting you down.

+ Your written communication skills will be tested in many assignments. Work at improving areas of weakness, such as spelling, punctuation or vocabulary.

+ You will be expected to work co-operatively with other people both at work and during many assignments. Be sensitive to other people's feelings, not just your own, and always be prepared to do your fair share of the work and help other people when you can.

+ To research effectively you need to know exactly what you are trying to find and where to look. This means understanding how reference media is stored in your library as well as how to search online. Good organisation skills also help so that you store important information carefully and can find it later. And never forget to include your sources in a bibliography.

+ Making a presentation requires several skills and may be nerve-racking at first. You will reduce your problems if you prepare well, are not too ambitious and have several run-throughs beforehand. Remember to speak clearly and a little more slowly than normal and smile from time to time!

ACTION POINTS

✓ Test both your numeracy and literacy skills at http://www.move-on.org.uk/testyourskills.asp# to check your current level. You don't need to register on the site if you click to do the 'mini-test' instead. If either need improvement, get help at http://www.bbc.co.uk/keyskills/it/1.shtml.

✓ Do the following two tasks with a partner to jerk your brain into action!

  – Each write down 36 simple calculations in a list, eg 8 x 6, 19 – 8, 14 + 6. Then exchange lists. See who can answer the most correctly in the shortest time.

  – Each write down 30 short random words (no more than 8 letters), eg cave, table, happily. Exchange lists. You each have three minutes to try to remember as many words as possible. Then hand back the list and write down all those you can recall. See who can remember the most.

✓ Assess your own keyboarding, proof-reading, document production, written communication and IT skills. Then find out if your tutors agree with you!

✓ List ten traits in other people that drive you mad. Then, for each one, suggest what you could do to cope with the problem (or solve it) rather than make a fuss. Compare your ideas with other members of your group.

✓ Take a note of all feedback you receive from your tutors, especially in relation to working with other people, researching and giving presentations. In each case focus on their suggestions and ideas so that you continually improve your skills throughout the course.

27

- Don't be over-ambitious. Take account of your timescale, resources and the skills of the team. Remember that a simple, clear presentation is often more professional than an over-elaborate or complicated one where half the visual aids don't work properly!

- If you are using PowerPoint try to avoid preparing every slide with bullet points! For variety, include some artwork and vary the designs. Remember that you should *never* just read your slides to the audience! Instead, prepare notes that you can print out that will enable you to enhance and extend what the audience is reading.

■ Your preparations should also include checking the venue and time; deciding what to wear and getting it ready; preparing, checking and printing any handouts; deciding what questions might be asked and how to answer these.

■ Have several run-throughs beforehand and check your timings. Check, too, that you can be heard clearly. This means lifting up your head and 'speaking' to the back of the room a little more slowly and loudly than you normally do.

■ On the day, arrive in plenty of time so that you aren't rushed or stressed. Remember that taking deep breaths helps to calm your nerves.

■ Start by introducing yourself clearly and smile at the audience. If it helps, find a friendly face and pretend you are just talking to that person.

■ Answer any questions honestly and don't exaggerate, guess or waffle. If you don't know the answer then say so!

■ If you are giving the presentation in a team, help out someone else who is struggling with a question if you know the answer.

■ Don't get annoyed or upset if you get any negative feedback afterwards. Instead, take note so that you can concentrate on improving your own performance next time. And don't focus on one or two criticisms and ignore all the praise you received! Building on the good and minimising the bad is how everyone improves in life!

STEP SEVEN

MAXIMISE YOUR OPPORTUNITIES AND MANAGE YOUR PROBLEMS

Like most things in life, you may have a few ups and downs on your course – particularly if you are studying over quite a long time, such as one or two years. Sometimes everything will be marvellous – you are enjoying all the units, you are up-to-date with your work, you are finding the subjects interesting and having no problems with any of your research tasks. At other times you may struggle a little more. You may find one or two topics rather tedious, or there may be distractions or worries in your personal life that you have to cope with. You may struggle to concentrate on the work and do your best.

Rather than just suffering in silence or gritting your teeth if things go a bit awry it is sensible if you have an action plan to help you cope. Equally, rather than just accepting good opportunities for additional experiences or learning, it is also wise to plan how to make the best of these. This section will show you how to do this.

Making the most of your opportunities

The following are examples of opportunities to find out more about information relevant to your course or to try putting some of your skills into practice.

- **External visits** You may go out of college on visits to different places or organisations. These are not days off – there is a reason for making each trip. Prepare in advance by reading relevant topics and make notes of useful information whilst you are there. Then write (or type) it up neatly as soon as you can and file it where you can find it again!

- **Visiting speakers** Again, people are asked to talk to your group for a purpose. You are likely to be asked to contribute towards questions that may be asked – which may be submitted in advance so that the speaker is clear on the topics you are studying. Think carefully about information that you would find helpful so that you can ask one or two relevant and useful questions. Take notes whilst the speaker is addressing your group, unless someone is recording the session. Be prepared to thank the speaker on behalf of your group if you are asked to do so.

- **Professional contacts** These will be the people you meet on work experience doing the real job that one day you hope to do. Make the most of meeting these people to find out about the vocational area of your choice.

- **Work experience** If you need to undertake practical work for any particular units of your BTEC National qualification, and if you are studying full-time, then your tutor will organise a work experience placement for you and talk to you about the evidence you need to obtain. You may also be issued with a special log book or diary in which to record your experiences. Before you start your placement, check that you are clear about all the details, such as the time you will start and leave, the name of your supervisor, what you should wear and what you should do if you are ill during the placement and cannot attend. Read and reread the units to which your evidence will apply and make sure you understand the grading criteria and what you need to obtain. Then make a note of appropriate headings to record your information. Try to make time to write up your notes, log book and/or diary every night, while your experiences are fresh in your mind.

- **In your own workplace** You may be studying your BTEC National qualification on a part-time basis and also have a full-time job in the same vocational area. Or you may be studying full-time and have a part-time job just to earn some money. In either case you should be alert to opportunities to find out more about topics that relate to your workplace, no matter how generally. For example, many BTEC courses include topics such as health and safety, teamwork, dealing with customers, IT security and communications – to name but a few. All these are topics that your employer will have had to address and finding out more about these will broaden your knowledge and help to give more depth to your assignment responses.

- **Television programmes, newspapers, Podcasts and other information sources** No matter what vocational area you are studying, the media are likely to be an invaluable source of information. You should be alert to any news bulletins that relate to your studies as well as relevant information in more topical television programmes. For example, if you are studying Art and Design then you should make a particular effort to watch the *Culture Show* as well as programmes on artists, exhibitions or other topics of interest. Business students should find inspiration by watching *Dragons Den*, *The Apprentice* and the *Money Programme* and Travel and Tourism students should watch holiday, travel and adventure programmes. If you are studying Media, Music and Performing Arts then you are spoiled for choice! Whatever your vocational choice, there will be television and radio programmes of special interest to you.

Remember that you can record television programmes to watch later if you prefer, and check out newspaper headlines online and from sites such as BBC news. The same applies to Podcasts. Of course, to know which information is relevant means that you must be familiar with the content of all the units you are studying, so it is useful to know what topics you will be learning about in the months to come, as well as the ones you are covering now. That way you can recognise useful opportunities when they arise.

The media are invaluable sources of information

Minimising problems

If you are fortunate, any problems you experience on your course will only be minor ones. For example, you may struggle to keep yourself motivated every single day and there may be times that you are having difficulty with a topic. Or you may be struggling to work with someone else in your team or to understand a particular tutor.

During induction you should have been told which tutor to talk to in this situation, and who to see if that person is absent or if you would prefer to see someone else. If you are having difficulties which are distracting you and affecting your work then it is sensible to ask to see your tutor promptly so that you can talk in confidence, rather than just trusting to luck everything will go right again. It is a rare student who is madly enthusiastic about every part of a course and all the other people on the course, so your tutor won't be surprised if you contact him/her and will be able to give you useful guidance to help you stay on track.

If you are very unlucky, you may have a more serious personal problem to deal with. In this case it is important that you know the main sources of help in your school or college and how to access these.

- **Professional counselling** There may be a professional counselling service if you have a concern that you don't want to discuss with any teaching staff. If you book an appointment to see a counsellor then you can be certain that nothing you say will ever be mentioned to another member of staff without your permission.

- **Student complaints procedures** If you have a serious complaint to make then the first step is to talk to a tutor, but you should be aware of the formal student complaints procedures that exist if you cannot resolve the problem informally. Note that these are only used for serious issues, not for minor difficulties.

- **Student appeals procedures** If you cannot agree with a tutor about a final grade for an assignment then you need to check the grading criteria and ask the tutor to explain how the grade was awarded. If you are still unhappy then you should see your personal tutor. If you still disagree then you have the right to make a formal appeal.

- **Student disciplinary procedures** These exist so that all students who flout the rules in a school or college will be dealt with in the same way. Obviously it is wise to avoid getting into trouble at any time, but, if you find yourself on the wrong side of the regulations, do read the procedures carefully to see what could happen. Remember that being honest about what happened and making a swift apology is always the wisest course of action, rather than being devious or trying to blame someone else.

- **Serious illness** Whether this affects you or a close family member, it could severely affect your attendance. The sooner you discuss the problem with your tutor the better. This is because you will be missing notes and information from the first day you do not attend. Many students underestimate the ability of their tutors to find inventive solutions in this type of situation – from sending notes by post to updating you electronically if you are well enough to cope with the work.

PLUSPOINTS

+ Some students miss out on opportunities to learn more about relevant topics. This may be because they haven't read the unit specifications, so don't know what topics they will be learning about in future; haven't prepared in advance or don't take advantage of occasions when they can listen to an expert and perhaps ask questions. Examples of these occasions include external visits, visiting speakers, work experience, being at work and watching television.

+ Many students encounter minor difficulties, especially if their course lasts a year or two. It is important to talk to your tutor, or another appropriate person, promptly if you have a worry that is affecting your work.

+ All schools and colleges have procedures for dealing with important issues and problems such as serious complaints, major illnesses, student appeals and disciplinary matters. It is important to know what these are.

ACTION POINTS

✓ List the type of opportunities available on your course for obtaining more information and talking to experts. Then check with your tutor to make sure you haven't missed out any.

✓ Check out the content of each unit you will be studying so that you know the main topics you have still to study.

✓ Identify the type of information you can find on television, in newspapers and in Podcasts that will be relevant to your studies.

✓ Check out your school or college documents and procedures to make sure that you know who to talk to in a crisis and who you can see if the first person is absent.

✓ Find out where you can read a copy of the main procedures in your school or college that might affect you if you have a serious problem. Then do so.

AND FINALLY . . .

Don't expect this Introduction to be of much use if you skim through it quickly and then put it to one side. Instead, refer to it whenever you need to remind yourself about something related to your course.

The same applies to the rest of this Student Guide. The Activities in the next section have been written to help you to demonstrate your understanding of many of the key topics contained in the core or specialist units you are studying. Your tutor may tell you to do these at certain times; otherwise there is nothing to stop you working through them yourself!

Similarly, the Marked Assignments in the final section have been written to show you how your assignments may be worded. You can also see the type of response that will achieve a Pass, Merit and Distinction – as well as the type of response that won't! Read these carefully and if any comment or grade puzzles you, ask your tutor to explain it.

Then keep this guide in a safe place so that you can use it whenever you need to refresh your memory. That way, you will get the very best out of your course – and yourself!

GLOSSARY

Note: all words highlighted in bold in the text are defined in the glossary.

Accreditation of Prior Learning (APL)

APL is an assessment process that enables your previous achievements and experiences to count towards your qualification providing your evidence is authentic, current, relevant and sufficient.

Apprenticeships

Schemes that enable you to work and earn money at the same time as you gain further qualifications (an **NVQ** award and a technical certificate) and improve your key skills. Apprentices learn work-based skills relevant to their job role and their chosen industry. You can find out more at www.apprenticeships.org.uk/

Assessment methods

Methods, such as **assignments**, case studies and practical tasks, used to check that your work demonstrates the learning and understanding required for your qualification.

Assessor

The tutor who marks or assesses your work.

Assignment

A complex task or mini-project set to meet specific **grading criteria**.

Awarding body

The organisation which is responsible for devising, assessing and issuing qualifications. The awarding body for all BTEC qualifications is Edexcel.

Core units

On a BTEC National course these are the compulsory or mandatory units that all students must complete to gain the qualification. Some BTEC qualifications have an over-arching title, eg Engineering, but within Engineering you can choose different routes. In this case you will study both common core units that are common to all engineering qualifications and **specialist core unit(s)** which are specific to your chosen **pathway**.

Degrees

These are higher education qualifications which are offered by universities and colleges. Foundation degrees take two years to complete; honours degrees may take three years or longer. See also **Higher National Certificates and Diplomas**.

DfES

The Department for Education and Skills: this is the government department responsible for education issues. You can find out more at www.dfes.gov.uk

Distance learning

This enables you to learn and/or study for a qualification without attending an Edexcel centre although you would normally be supported by a member of staff who works there. You communicate with your tutor and/or the centre that organises the distance learning programme by post, telephone or electronically.

Educational Maintenance Award (EMA)

This is a means-tested award which provides eligible students under 19, who are studying a full-time course at school or college, with a cash sum of money every week. See http://www.dfes.gov.uk/financialhelp/ema/ for up-to-date details.

External verification

Formal checking by a representative of Edexcel of the way a BTEC course is delivered. This includes sampling various assessments to check content and grading.

Final major project

This is a major, individual piece of work that is designed to enable you to demonstrate you have achieved several learning outcomes for a BTEC National qualification in the creative or performing arts. Like all assessments, this is internally assessed.

Forbidden combinations

Qualifications or units that cannot be taken simultaneously because their content is too similar.

GLH

See **Guided Learning Hours** on page 34.

Grade

The rating (Pass, Merit or Distinction) given to the mark you have obtained which identifies the standard you have achieved.

Grade boundaries

The pre-set points at which the total points you have earned for different units converts to the overall grade(s) for your qualification.

Grading criteria

The standard you have to demonstrate to obtain a particular grade in the unit, in other words, what you have to prove you can do.

Grading domains

The main areas of learning which support the **learning outcomes**. On a BTEC National course these are: application of knowledge and understanding; development of practical and technical skills; personal development for occupational roles; application of generic and **key skills**. Generic skills are basic skills needed wherever you work, such as the ability to work cooperatively as a member of a team.

Grading grid

The table in each unit of your BTEC qualification specification that sets out the **grading criteria**.

Guided Learning Hours (GLH)

The approximate time taken to deliver a unit which includes the time taken for direct teaching, instruction and assessment and for you to carry out directed assignments or directed individual study. It does not include any time you spend on private study or researching an assignment. The GLH determines the size of the unit. At BTEC National level, units are either 30, 60, 90 or 120 guided learning hours. By looking at the number of GLH a unit takes, you can see the size of the unit and how long it is likely to take you to learn and understand the topics it contains.

Higher education (HE)

Post-secondary and post-further education, usually provided by universities and colleges.

Higher-level skills

Skills such as evaluating or critically assessing complex information that are more difficult than lower level skills such as writing a description or making out a list. You must be able to demonstrate higher level skills to achieve a Distinction grade.

Higher National Certificates and Diplomas

Higher National Certificates and Diplomas are vocational qualifications offered at colleges around the country. Certificates are part-time and designed to be studied by people who are already in work; students can use their work experiences to build on their learning. Diplomas are full-time courses – although often students will spend a whole year on work experience part way through their Diploma. Higher Nationals are roughly equivalent to half a degree.

Indicative reading

Recommended books and journals whose content is both suitable and relevant for the unit.

Induction

A short programme of events at the start of a course designed to give you essential information and introduce you to your fellow students and tutors so that you can settle down as quickly and easily as possible.

Internal verification

The quality checks carried out by nominated tutor(s) at your school or college to ensure that all assignments are at the right level and cover appropriate learning outcomes. The checks also ensure that all **assessors** are marking work consistently and to the same standard.

Investors in People (IIP)

A national quality standard which sets a level of good practice for the training and development of people. Organisations must demonstrate their commitment to achieve the standard.

Key skills

The transferable, essential skills you need both at work and to run your own life successfully. They are: literacy, numeracy, IT, problem solving, working with others and self-management.

Learning and Skills Council (LSC)

The government body responsible for planning and funding education and training for everyone aged over 16 in England – except university students. You can find out more at www.lsc.gov.uk

Learning outcomes

The knowledge and skills you must demonstrate to show that you have effectively learned a unit.

Learning support

Additional help that is available to all students in a school or college who have learning difficulties or other special needs. These include reasonable adjustments to help to reduce the effect of a disability or difficulty that would place a student at a substantial disadvantage in an assessment situation.

Levels of study

The depth, breadth and complexity of knowledge, understanding and skills required to achieve a qualification determines its level. Level 2 is broadly equivalent to GCSE level (grades A*-C) and level 3 equates to GCE level. As you successfully achieve one level, you can then progress on to the next. BTEC qualifications are offered at Entry level, then levels 1, 2, 3, 4 and 5.

Local Education Authority (LEA)

The local government body responsible for providing education for students of compulsory school age in your area.

Mentor

A more experienced person who will guide and counsel you if you have a problem or difficulty.

Mode of delivery

The way in which a qualification is offered to students, eg part-time, full-time, as a short course or by **distance learning**.

National Occupational Standard (NOS)

These are statements of the skills, knowledge and understanding you need to develop to be competent at a particular job. These are drawn up by the **Sector Skills Councils**.

National Qualification Framework (NQF)

The framework into which all accredited qualifications in the UK are placed. Each is awarded a level based on their difficulty which ensures that all those at the same level are of the same standard. (See also **levels of study**.)

National Vocational Qualification (NVQ)

Qualifications which concentrate upon the practical skills and knowledge required to do a job competently. They are usually assessed in the workplace and range from level 1 (the lowest) to level 5 (the highest).

Nested qualifications

Qualifications which have 'common' units, so that students can easily progress from one to another by adding on more units, such as the BTEC Award, BTEC Certificate and BTEC Diploma.

Pathway

All BTEC National qualifications are comprised of a small number of core units and a larger number of specialist units. These specialist units are grouped into different combinations to provide alternative pathways to achieving the qualification, linked to different career preferences.

Peer review

An occasion when you give feedback on the performance of other members in your team and they, in turn, comment on your performance.

Plagiarism

The practice of copying someone else's work and passing it off as your own. *This is strictly forbidden on all courses.*

Portfolio

A collection of work compiled by a student, usually as evidence of learning to produce for an **assessor**.

Professional body

An organisation that exists to promote or support a particular profession, such as the Law Society and the Royal Institute of British Architects.

Professional development and training

Activities that you can undertake, relevant to your job, that will increase and/or update your knowledge and skills.

Project

A comprehensive piece of work which normally involves original research and investigation either by an individual or a team. The findings and results may be presented in writing and summarised in a presentation.

Qualifications and Curriculum Authority (QCA)

The public body, sponsored by the **DfES**, responsible for maintaining and developing the national curriculum and associated assessments, tests and examinations. It also accredits and monitors qualifications in colleges and at work. You can find out more at www.qca.gov.uk

Quality assurance

In education, this is the process of continually checking that a course of study is meeting the specific requirements set down by the awarding body.

Sector Skills Councils (SSCs)

The 25 employer-led, independent organisations that are responsible for improving workforce skills in the UK by identifying skill gaps and improving learning in the workplace. Each council covers a different type of industry and develops its **National Occupational Standards**.

Semester

Many universities and colleges divide their academic year into two halves or semesters, one from September to January and one from February to July.

Seminar

A learning event between a group of students and a tutor. This may be student-led, following research into a topic which has been introduced earlier.

Specialist core units

See under **Core units**.

Study buddy

A person in your group or class who takes notes for you and keeps you informed of important developments if you are absent. You do the same in return.

Time-constrained assignment

An assessment you must complete within a fixed time limit.

Tutorial

An individual or small group meeting with your tutor at which you can discuss the work you are currently doing and other more general course issues. At an individual tutorial your progress on the course will be discussed and you can also raise any concerns or personal worries you have.

The University and Colleges Admissions Service (UCAS)

The central organisation which processes all applications for higher education courses. You pronounce this 'You-Cass'.

UCAS points

The number of points allocated by **UCAS** for the qualifications you have obtained. **HE** institutions specify how many points you need to be accepted on the courses they offer. You can find out more at www.ucas.com

Unit abstract

The summary at the start of each BTEC unit that tells you what the unit is about.

Unit content

Details about the topics covered by the unit and the knowledge and skills you need to complete it.

Unit points

The number of points you have gained when you complete a unit. These depend upon the grade you achieve (Pass, Merit or Distinction) and the size of the unit as determined by its **guided learning hours**.

Vocational qualification

A qualification which is designed to develop the specific knowledge and understanding relevant to a chosen area of work.

Work experience

Any time you spend on an employer's premises when you carry out work-based tasks as an employee but also learn about the enterprise and develop your skills and knowledge.

ACTIVITIES

UNIT 1 – Communication and Employability   **40**
       Skills for IT

UNIT 2 – Computer Systems   **55**

UNIT 3 – Information Systems   **77**

UNIT 15 – Organisational Systems Security   **93**

This section focuses on grading criteria P1, P6, P7; M4 and D2 from Unit 1 – Communication and Employability Skills for IT.

Learning outcomes

1 Understand the attributes of employees that are valued by employers.

4 Be able to identify personal development needs and the ways of addressing them.

Content

1) **Understand the attributes of employees that are valued by employers**

   Specific job-related: technical knowledge; working procedures and systems including health and safety.

   General: planning and organisational skills; time management; team working; verbal and written communication skills; numeric skills; other, eg creativity.

   Attitudes: determined; independent; working with integrity; tolerant; dependable; problem-solving; other, eg leadership, confidence, self-motivation.

   Organisational aims and objectives: general as relevant to all employees; specific as relevant to the role of individuals; responsibilities of the individual in promoting organisational brand or image.

4) **Be able to identify personal development needs and the ways of addressing them**

   Identification of needs: self-assessment; formal reports, eg following appraisal meetings; other, eg customer feedback, performance data.

   Records: personal development plans including target setting; other, eg appraisal records.

   Methods of addressing needs: job shadowing, formal courses or training (external, internal); other, eg team meetings, attending events.

   Learning styles: examples of systems, eg active/reflective, sensing/intuitive, visual/verbal, sequential/global; identification of preferred style; how to benefit from knowing your learning style; understanding how other people's learning styles impact on team working.

Grading criteria

P1 explain why employers value particular employee attributes

In order to meet this criterion you will need to understand how job seekers can 'sell' themselves to future employers and why the job seeker needs certain skills and attributes.

P6 describe ways of identifying and meeting development needs

For this criterion you may be asked to identify training and development needs in a particular organisation and show how these might be met.

M4 explain how individuals can use a knowledge of their learning style to improve their effectiveness in developing new skills or understanding

Assessment for this could come in the form of a report and could possibly be an extension of the training and development needs.

P7 create and maintain a personal development plan

D2 independently use a personal development plan to undergo a process of identification of skill-need and related improvement

The evidence for these will be your own personal development plan which you will set up at the start of the course, keep maintained and summarise at the end (P7). Your plan will include setting targets. You will keep track of everything that your teachers ask you to learn and to improve. If you are in employment you can add detail from your employer. If you undertake any voluntary work or belong to any organisations such as the TA, Cadets or Scouts then aspects from these can also be added. To reach the D2 distinction level you must have proof that you have kept to the plan and followed it all by yourself. This can come in the form of statements from your teachers, employers or group leaders.

HEALTH AND SAFETY AT WORK

All workers have a right to work in places where risks to their health and safety are properly controlled. The primary responsibility for this is down to the employer. Workers have a right to join and be represented by a trade union. Both workers and employers have a legal responsibility to look after health and safety-at-work together. Workers who contribute to health and safety at work are safer – and possibly healthier – than those who do not.

ACTIVITY 1

Individually, go to the following website http://www.hse.gov.uk/index.htm and find out about the legislation involving health and safety at work (as it relates to IT use). Write a concise report of your findings (150 words) and report back to the class to discuss general issues.

ACTIVITY 2

Task 1

In small groups, walk around the computer rooms in your school or college and identify:

- how the Health and Safety Executive (HSE) guidelines are being met
- where there are issues that need resolving
- how these issues might be resolved.

Report your findings back to the class as a whole.

Task 2

If you have a job, repeat the above activity at your workplace and prepare a report for your managers covering all three points.

Task 3

In pairs, visit your local DIY store or garden centre, look for areas where the health-and-safety guidelines may not be met. Write a summary of areas for improvement.

JOB SEEKING

When applying for jobs it is important that you understand what the prospective employer is looking for. If you have a part-time job you will already have some understanding of this topic. How does the employer choose one candidate over another? How can you make sure that you always meet the employer's needs in the job role? How can you learn about the job and all the aspects entailed (specific to your level in the organisation)?

ACTIVITY 3

Task 1

Working in small groups, make sure that at least one person in your group has, or has had, a part-time job, and complete a copy of the following table for that person:

Job-specific skills	Knowledge required
Technical knowledge	
Working procedures involved including health and safety issues	

Report your findings back to the class and find the common aspects.

Task 2

Get back in the same groups and repeat the exercise for this job specification.

This job is ideal for someone with recent relevant experience or qualifications looking to start or develop their IT career. The right candidate will have plenty of opportunity to develop within the role and become a key member of the IT team.

The job:

- Front-line troubleshooting and support for users, PCs, printers and photocopiers.
- Installation and maintenance of hardware and software.
- Operating back-up system.
- Testing software and researching new packages.
- Supporting and training users in the use of bespoke software, as well as Microsoft Office applications.

Knowledge:

- Recent experience and/or qualifications in IT.
- Knowledge of Windows 98/2000/XP/2003.
- Sound understanding of Microsoft Office applications.
- Experience of Sophos Anti-virus, Backup Exec and Active Directory.

Job-specific skills	Knowledge required
Technical knowledge	
Working procedures involved including health and safety issues	

Report your findings back to the class and find the common aspects.

ACTIVITY 4

Task 1

Working individually, rate your personal skills, in a copy of the table below; show where there are areas for improvement and what you might do to improve your skills.

Use the following ratings: 1 excellent, 2 good, 3 average, 4 poor, 5 non-existent.

Skills	Rating	Areas for improvement	Techniques for improvement
Planning Organisational Time management			
Team working			
Verbal communication Written communication Numeric skills Creativity			

Save the results of this exercise as you can use them for another activity in this unit.

Task 2

Following the previous activity, discuss with your teacher your personal findings and decisions so that you can look to maintain and improve your skills.

ACTIVITY 5

Task 1

Working in small groups and using the following job specification, rate the skills the employer is looking for. Give reasons for your decisions.

This job is ideal for someone with recent relevant experience or qualifications looking to start or develop their IT career. The right candidate will have plenty of opportunity to develop within the role and become a key member of the IT team.

The job:

- Front-line troubleshooting and support for users, PCs, printers and photocopiers.
- Installation and maintenance of hardware and software.

43

- Operating back-up system.
- Testing software and researching new packages.
- Supporting and training users in the use of bespoke software, as well as Microsoft Office applications.

The person:

- A passion for IT and its use in business.
- The ideal candidate will be self-motivated, dependable, responsible and able to work unsupervised.

Use the following ratings: 1 excellent, 2 good, 3 average, 4 poor, 5 not important.

Skills	Rating	Areas for improvement	Techniques for improvement
Planning Organisational Time management			
Team working			
Verbal communication Written communication Numeric skills Creativity			

Task 2

Apart from those skills that can be quantified, you will also have more personal and people-related skills. Working individually, rate your personal skills, in a copy of the table below, and show where there are areas for improvement and what you might do to improve your skills.

Use the following ratings: 1 excellent, 2 good, 3 average, 4 poor, 5 non-existent.

Skills	Rating	Areas for improvement	Techniques for improvement
Determination			
Independence			
Integrity			
Tolerance			
Dependability			
Problem solving			
Leadership			
Confidence			
Self-motivation			

Save the results of this exercise as you can make use of them later in another activity.

Task 3

Following the previous activity, discuss with your teacher your personal findings and decisions so that you can look to maintain and improve your skills.

Task 4

In small groups, complete copies of the three tables for the following job specification. Report your findings back to the class.

An IT Assistant is required for a leading manufacturer and supplier of scientific consumables at their UK office. The following are essential to the position:

- Ability to earn trust and respect from colleagues
- Desire to learn and support all aspects of IT infrastructure and operational administration
- Outstanding drive and ambition
- Keen and demonstrable personal interest in IT
- Willingness to travel.

Initially, the successful candidate will work on the IT support helpdesk, learning about the company's systems, structures and procedures. The individual will receive training in IT security processes at the same time, and will transfer to being a full-time Security Specialist in 6–12 months.

Use the following ratings: 1 excellent, 2 good, 3 average, 4 poor, 5 not important.

Skills	Rating	Justification of rating in relation to job specification
Planning		
Organisational		
Time management		
Team working		
Verbal communication		
Written communication		
Numeric skills		
Creativity		

Job-specific skills	Knowledge required	Justification of decisions
Technical knowledge		
Working procedures involved including health and safety issues		

Skills	Rating	Areas for improvement	Techniques for improvement
Determination			
Independence			
Integrity			
Tolerance			
Dependability			
Problem solving			
Leadership			
Confidence			
Self-motivation			

ACTIVITY 6

Write a brief report (no more than 300 words) identifying the skills, knowledge and attributes that this employer might expect in the applicant. Give brief reasons for your decisions. You will meet a task like this in the exemplar assignment that accompanies this section.

The client, a leading software services organisation, requires a 1st line helpdesk assistant to join their award-winning team. You will act as the first point of contact for all helpdesk calls. Daily duties would involve logging the calls, ensuring that each call is checked, updated and progressed accordingly, whilst adhering to company SLA agreements. Knowledge of Remote Support, VNC, MS Word, Outlook and Windows 98 or later is essential and any IT qualifications will be very beneficial. You should have excellent written and oral communication skills, a good telephone manner and call management experience, be personable and presentable and should have a proven track record as a strong team player. This is an excellent entry-evel opportunity with long-term career prospects.

ACTIVITY 7

Task 1

Interview the technician who works in the computing area of your school or college and get them to identify their personal skills, attributes and technical knowledge and understanding of the job. Ask the technician to tell you what they had to find out and where they had to develop skills when they joined the organisation.

Task 2

If possible, ask your teacher to provide you with the job specification for the technician's job. Working in small groups, identify the differences between the technician's and the organisation's view of the job. Report your findings back to the class and discuss.

ACTIVITY 8

Task 1

This activity builds on the issues raised in the previous section and will help you decide how you might want to develop your skills and attributes. Individually, investigate Belbin's team roles using the following website, http://www.belbin.info/belbin_career_planning.htm

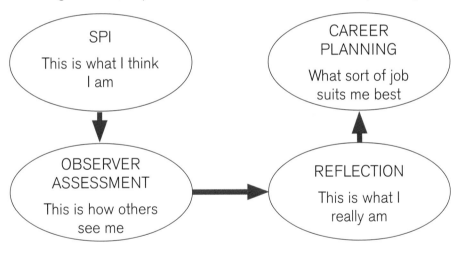

Task 2

Now rate yourself and see what sort of person you are. Use the following ratings against each bullet point in each section of the table:
1 excellent, 2 good, 3 average, 4 poor, 5 non-existent.

Strengths and styles	How do I rate myself?	Role name
• Able to get others working to a shared aim • Confident • Mature		Co-ordinator (CO)
• Motivated • Energetic • Achievement-driven • Assertive • Competitive		Shaper (SH)
• Innovative • Inventive • Creative • Original • Imaginative • Unorthodox • Problem-solving		Plant (PL)
• Serious • Prudent • Critical thinker • Analytical		Monitor–Evaluator (ME)
• Systematic • Common sense • Loyal • Structured • Reliable • Dependable • Practical • Efficient		Implementer (IMP)
• Quick, good communicator • Outgoing • Affable • Seeks and finds options • Negotiator		Resource Investigator (RI)
• Supportive • Sociable • Flexible • Adaptable • Perceptive • Listener • Calming • Influence • Mediator		Team Worker (TW)

Strengths and styles	How do I rate myself?	Role name
• Attention to detail • Accurate • High standards • Quality orientated • Delivers to schedule and specification		Completer–Finisher (CF)
• Technical expert • Highly focused capability and knowledge • Driven by professional standards • Dedication to personal subject area		Specialist (SP)

Then add up the scores in each section and convert them into a percentage based on the number of options per section – the lowest section percentage score will indicate the type of person that you might be when in employment. You will be able to use this in developing your personal development plan (see Activity 13).

Task 3

If you have a part-time or voluntary job (or are in the TA, Cadets or Scouts), take your results to your supervisor; ask them to confirm or refute the results. Ask them for reasons for their ideas on your skills and attributes.

Task 4

Now put it all into practice. Have a look for job specifications in the local newspaper that ask for trainee IT support staff. Practise writing job applications stressing your strengths and disguising your weaknesses (without fabricating too much). Ask your communications staff at school or college to review your work.

TRAINING AND DEVELOPMENT NEEDS

The need for training and staff development should be at the heart of the development of any business. Lack of it can cause staff to leave because of low moral; the organisation may not perform at its best because staff do not know how to use equipment properly or are not sure what the correct procedure is or because staff have not been given the opportunity to update their skills or knowledge. It is also important to know what training and development each member of staff should undertake to help them perform their job effectively and also remain up to date with legislation, procedures, software and hardware. Training can take many forms and last different lengths of time depending on the immediate and long-term needs of the individual and the organisation. The employer should not necessarily expect that the individual will know what is best for them so plans need to be drawn up for each person concerned.

ACTIVITY 9

Task 1

Using the Internet, investigate Investors in People. Find out why organisations are so keen to sign up to it. What are the aspects that organisations must achieve before they are awarded the IIP quality certificate?

Task 2

Find out if your school or college has signed up and has the right to use the IIP logo.

Task 3

Using Yell.com, or similar sources, make up a list of local medium-sized and large employers. Find out whether they have signed up for IIP. Identify the main function of the organisation (eg IT, bakery, etc).

Organisation	IIP?	Function

ACTIVITY 10

Task 1

Again, use the Internet to see if there is any legislation that must be adhered to when providing training and development. Write a brief report summarising anything you think is appropriate.

Task 2

Search the web for training establishments that focus on IT skills. Find a list of six or so; see what these organisations have in common, what sort of courses they offer, what legislation they follow (eg Data Protection), whether they offer any courses that you might be interested in following (if you could afford them!), what courses might enhance your studies at school or college. Copy and complete the following table:

Establishment	Courses offered	Legislation followed	Interested in doing and why	Common features

ACTIVITY 11

Using the following website as a basis, ignoring the specific references to QAA, http://www.qaa.ac.uk/aboutus/policy/ TrainingDevelopmentPolicy.asp, discuss with your class colleagues how you would expect to decide on a training plan for yourself. Decide who you would ask for advice, who could help you and who would determine your training needs.

LEARNING STYLES

What are learning styles? Many academicians have written theories on this topic. A learning style will describe the traits and techniques you use when you have to get and understand new knowledge.

ACTIVITY 12

Task 1

Working individually, using the website http://www.emtech.net/ learning_theories.htm, investigate different learning styles reviewed over the years. Discuss your findings with the rest of the class.

Task 2

Working in pairs, complete the following quiz, once for yourself then for your colleague. When trainers are designing courses for others it is important that they have an understanding of how people learn and assimilate new knowledge. Following that, training courses can then be provided that address the needs of all learners.

Do not take a long time to complete the quiz but, instead, answer instinctively. Too much thought can make you change your mind too often!

Aspect	Choices	You	Your colleague
When you are reading, do you	A Visualise in your mind the descriptive passages? B Enjoy the characters' dialogue? C Sometimes read action stories, but would prefer not to read?		
You can remember a list of items best if you	A Write them down. B Recite the list to yourself. C Use your fingers to count the items off.		
When problem solving, you	A Write the problem down or draw diagrams to visualise it. B Talk to someone (or yourself) about it. C Try and use concrete objects to find a solution.		
When you are spelling, do you	A Try to 'see' the word? B Sound the word out before or as you spell it? C Write the word down to find out if it looks or 'feels' right?		
When learning something new, you	A Like to have the aid of diagrams, posters, or a demonstration. B Like to have verbal instructions. C Just go for it and try it out!		
When trying to recall names, do you remember	A The person's face but not their name? B The person's name but not their face? C Clearly the situation in which you met them?		
If you need help with a particular computer application, would you	A Look for pictures or diagrams to explain the solution? B Ask someone for help or call a help desk? C Persevere and try to figure it out yourself?		
If you are putting something together, you	A Follow the instructions and look at the pictures. B Wish there was a video or tape explaining what to do. C Ignore the instructions and figure it out as you go!		
When concentrating on something, you	A Are distracted by movement and untidiness around you. B Are distracted by noises in the area you're working in. C Have difficulty sitting still for even short periods of time.		
When giving directions to someone, you	A Visualise the route first or draw a map. B Give clear, concise instructions. C Move your body and gesture as you give them.		

Aspect	Choices	You	Your colleague
When you are talking, do you have favourite words such as:	A See, picture and imagine. B Hear, tune and think. C Feel, touch and hold.		
When dealing with people at college or school with regard to your work, do you	A Prefer direct, face-to-face, personal meetings? B Prefer the telephone? C Talk with them while walking or participating in an activity?		

Choose one option from each list for yourself and for your colleague.

Task 3

Now you have completed the quiz, examine the results. Add the total number of responses for each letter (A, B, C) and record each total

You   A _____   B _____   C _____

Your colleague   A _____   B _____   C _____

Many people have more than one learning style so you may find you have some responses in each category. The category with the greater number of responses may be your (or your colleague's) main learning style.

If the majority of the responses were for A you are a visual learner.

If the majority of the responses were for B you are an auditory learner.

If the majority of the responses were for C you are a kinesthetic learner.

Task 4

If you want to check this out again try the quiz on the following website:

http://www.learning-styles-online.com/inventory/questions. asp?cookieset=y

Did you get the same answers?

PERSONAL DEVELOPMENT PLANNING

Your personal development plan (PDP) should consist of:

- short-term targets – these could be stepping stones to enable you to achieve your medium-term priorities, for instance, training to update and strengthen your skills. Generally these are things that can be achieved within the next 12 months
- medium-term plans – these should state your personal and business goals for the next two to five years
- long-term plan – this could ultimately be a life-time plan that includes your ultimate goals in both your personal and professional life.

You should also include a CV, that you update on a regular basis, and a list of all your academic and non-academic achievements, skills and experiences should be in there too.

ACTIVITY 13

Task 1

Log onto the Internet site http://www.leeds.ac.uk/textiles/keynote/ Keynote_PDP_portal/downloads.htm and open the file keynote_PDP. zip; in there you will find a series of documents that will help you create your own customised personal development plan. Read these documents carefully to see what they contain.

Task 2

With the help of your teacher and colleagues in the class, decide on a structure for a PDP that you will feel comfortable using. If it is not easy to use you will lose momentum to carry on using it. Failure to use your PDP will mean that you will not achieve criterion P7.

Task 3

Create an electronic version of your PDP and start to fill it out.

Task 4

Remember to look at your log and add to it on a regular basis.

UNIT 2 – COMPUTER SYSTEMS

This section focuses on grading criteria P1, P2, P3, P4, P5; M1, M2, M3; D1 and D2 from Unit 2 – Computer Systems.

Learning outcomes

1 Understand the hardware components of computer systems.

2 Understand the software components of computer systems.

3 Be able to undertake routine computer maintenance.

Content

1) **Understand the hardware components of computer systems**

   System unit components: processors and options; motherboard; BIOS; power supply; fan and heat sink; hard drive configuration and controllers, eg IDE, EIDE, master, slave; ports, eg USB, parallel, serial; peripherals, eg printer, camera, scanner, plotter; internal memory (RAM, ROM, cache); specialised cards, eg network, graphic cards.

   Backing store: types, eg disks, pen drives, optical media, flash memory cards; portable and fixed drives; performance factors, eg data transfer rate, capacity.

   Data transmission: communication paths, eg buses; modems; processor speed (impact on use, potential for overclocking); RAM speed; impact of transmission media.

   Considerations for selection: cost; user requirements, eg software to be used, need for maintenance contract, outputs required, need for integration with other systems such as home entertainment, processing power, storage capacity; accessibility for disabled users.

2) **Understand the software components of computer systems**

   Operating system software: operating system examples, eg LINUX, Windows, MAC OS; command line and GUI operating systems; operating system functions and services, eg machine and peripheral management, security, file management; device drivers.

   Software utilities: virus protection; firewalls; clean-up tools, eg for cookies, Internet history, defragmentation; drive formatting.

3) **Be able to undertake routine computer maintenance**

   Software maintenance: upgrade software, eg virus definition files; installation of patches; scheduling of maintenance tasks; utility software aimed at users, eg defragmentation, clean-up, system profilers; other third party utility software, eg compression utilities, spyware removal.

   Hardware maintenance: cleaning equipment; install and configure new peripherals, eg printers; install and configure additional or replacement device, eg hard drive, graphics card, sound card, optical media, network interface card; other issues, eg regulatory requirements risks, health and safety issues.

   File management: create folders; back-up procedures; others, eg delete files.

Grading criteria

P1 explain the function of the system unit components and how they communicate

This means that you will need to understand the role of each component inside the system unit (listed in *System unit components* section of Content) of a typical personal computer, how they communicate with each other and how data is moved between them as described in the section of Content for *Data transmission*. There should be a backup system as in the *Backing store* section of Content. It is possible that everything could be identified within one diagram.

Evidence for P1 could be:

■   demonstrating to your tutor how components are connected inside a system unit, showing how data is passed between them and documenting all questions and answers

- diagrams or photographs of the system unit with clear written explanations
- a presentation, showing the speaker's notes and/or a statement from someone in the audience
- a short test. If a test is used, however, you must show competence in all areas of the unit Content *System unit components*
- a web page with hot-spots over different components that explain what the components are. The communication between components must be identified.

P2 describe the purpose, features and functions of two different operating systems

This means that you will need to describe the purpose of two different operating systems along with their features and functions as found in *Operating system software* section of Content. Detailed descriptions of the operating systems do not need to be included to achieve P2, but are needed to achieve M2.

Evidence for P2 could be:

- a presentation with speaker notes and/or a statement from someone who heard the presentation
- a written report
- a table in a Word document describing the purpose, features and functions of two different operating systems.

P3 demonstrate the operation and explain the use of two different software utilities

To achieve P3, you will need to be hands-on, and to demonstrate operating two different utilities by actually using them. This will help you explain your use of two different software utilities you choose from the *Software utilities* section of Content.

Evidence for P3 could be:

- demonstrating your use of the two different software utilities to your tutor and documenting all of the questions and answers
- notes that you wrote as you used the utilities
- observation records, supported by someone who watched you use the utilities and then signed by your tutor
- a written report.

P4 describe the range of available utility software

There are four categories of utility identified in the *Software utilities* section of Content and you must describe an example of each. You may use a table in a document with enough information to describe what you've discovered about each of these four types of utility.

Evidence for P4 could be:

- a written report
- a table in a Word document describing four software utilities.

P5 undertake routine maintenance tasks in relation to a PC

You need to undertake at least one routine maintenance task on a personal computer from *each* of the sections of Content dealing with Software, Hardware maintenance *and* File management.

Evidence for P5 could be:

- demonstrating a routine maintenance task to your tutor and documenting all questions and answers and/or writing notes as you used the utilities
- observation records, supported by someone watching you use the utilities and then signed by your tutor
- notes that you wrote as you undertook the routine maintenance tasks
- a handwritten entry on a page of a maintenance log with supporting evidence from an observation record or your own notes on what you did.

M1 explain and implement the installation and configuration of an additional or replacement device

You will need to implement a practical activity or demonstration to install and configure a device into a computer system with an explanation. The device could be additional to the system or a replacement for an existing component. This could be based upon your P5 tasks with extra questioning and answers to show your understanding of the upgrade.

Evidence for M1 could be:

- demonstration to your tutor with documented questions and answers
- presentation with speaker notes and/or notes from someone who saw your presentation

- a written report
- supporting notes based on an observation record.

M2 compare the features and functions of two different operating systems

You need to build on your P2 evidence to include more detail by comparing the features and functions of two different operating systems as listed in the *Operating system software* section of Content. You need to write a summary of their respective strengths and weaknesses and compare them against each other.

Evidence for M2 could be:

- a presentation with your speaker's notes and/or a statement from someone who heard you give your presentation
- a written report
- a table in a Word document comparing the strengths and weaknesses of the features and functions of two different operating systems.

M3 explain the effect of the software maintenance activities carried out on the performance of a computer system

This means that you will need to be able to document the performance of a computer system before, and after, some maintenance to identify any differences. You will then be able to explain the effect of the software maintenance activities that you carried out on the performance of a computer system. This could be based upon your P5 tasks with extra questions and answers to show your understanding. Records of the performance of the software 'before and after' your maintenance could also be used as evidence for this criteria.

Evidence for M3 could be:

- demonstration of how the performance of a computer system was measured before, and after, some maintenance to identify any differences to your tutor with documented questions and answers
- written 'before and after' records.

D1 evaluate at least three specifications for commercially available computer systems and justify the one most suitable for use in a given situation

This means that you will need to have a defined scenario where the system is to be used, perhaps within a case study or from real life. A detailed requirements-list from this scenario would allow you to make an appropriate choice and be the basis for justifying your choice.

Three specifications for commercially available computer systems need to be found from the Internet or local retail outlets. You should evaluate these three specifications by referring back to the requirements-list and considering cost to identify how suitable they are for the given situation. See *Considerations for selection* section of Content for more guidance.

Evidence for D1 could be:

- presentation with speaker notes and/or a statement from someone who heard the presentation
- a written report.

D2 justify the considerations for selection in the upgrade of an existing computer system

This means you will need to justify what components you considered when selecting the upgrade of an existing computer system for P5 evidence as listed in the *Software* and *Hardware maintenance* sections of Content.

Evidence for D2 could be:

- a presentation, showing your speaking notes and/or a statement from someone in the audience
- a written report.

HARDWARE

ACTIVITY 1

You work part-time in a local computer shop on the counter and also assist in building and repairing PCs. The owner has asked you to produce a poster for the shop to help potential customers understand how PC components function and communicate with each other.

Use Google to search the *Images* pages with *computer system unit* as the search phrase. Choose some clear images that you are able to use to explain these components of a computer system:

- motherboard with
  - BIOS
  - buses
  - USB port
  - hard drive controller
  - RAM
  - processor
  - fan and heat sink
- case with power supply
- hard drive
- optical drive
- graphic card
- printer.

Use your images to create a poster showing the role of each of the components inside the system unit of a typical personal computer. Show how they communicate with each other and how data is moved between them.

The poster should also show where the external devices connect to the system unit.

The components should be clearly named on the poster with text to identify what data these devices communicate to each other.

ACTIVITY 2

You work on the shop counter of an independent computer shop. The owner has decided to hold an open evening on the first Monday of each month where the public are invited into the shop to see the range of products (with no sales pressure and a free buffet!). As part of these evenings there is to be a presentation on how each of the components in a computer system contributes to its workings.

Research the function of each of these components in a computer system (eg the function of a bus is to carry binary data between components):

- motherboard with
  - BIOS
  - buses
  - USB port

- - hard drive controller
  - RAM
  - processor
  - fan and heat sink
- power supply
- hard drive
- optical drive
- graphic card
- printer.

Find an appropriate image for each component.

Use your images to create a presentation with pages showing the function role of each component inside the system unit of a typical personal computer.

ACTIVITY 3

You work as a junior analyst-programmer in the IT Services section of a large company. One of the roles of your section is to recommend new IT purchases to the financial director (FD) for approval. The FD has asked IT Services to produce a report to help him understand why the components are needed and how they affect system performance. You have been given the task of producing the report.

Research the specification of a named example of each of these components in a computer system (eg the specification of a hard disk would include the cache size, spin speed, seek time, data transfer rate and ribbon cable interface type):

- motherboard
- processor and fan
- power supply
- hard drive
- optical drive
- graphic card
- external disk
- printer
- camera
- scanner.

Find appropriate images for all of the components.

Insert your images into a document, each with a specification summary for the component and written explanation of how the specification affects performance.

Useful websites include:

www.ebuyer.co.uk

www.dabs.com

www.maplin.co.uk

www.pcworld.co.uk

www.smart-computers.net

ACTIVITY 4

Your teacher/tutor has asked the class to produce some web pages that can be used for 'taster' days and to support the group for assignment evidence. The web pages are to explain how the components inside a computer system work.

Your teacher/tutor – or individual groups – should decide how to co-ordinate web pages so that all of the components are covered.

Use websites like the ones below (or a site of your own choice) to research how one of these components in a computer system works:

- motherboard with processor and fan
- power supply
- hard drive
- optical drive
- graphic card
- external disk
- printer
- camera
- scanner.

Useful sites might be:

www.howstuffworks.com/

www.houghtonmifflinbooks.com/features/davidmacaulay/

You should find appropriate images for all of these components, showing clearly how each of them works.

Task 1

Use your chosen image to create a web page showing an illustration of the component with a written explanation of how it works.

Task 2

Produce a website with links to the pages produced for the other components by other members of the class.

ACTIVITY 5

You work for a computer gaming centre in the IT Support section as a junior technician. The gaming centre has a public area where clients can hire PCs for network games singly or as a group. The centre also has offices used for administration and marketing as well as a network server room.

After a very successful year, the centre has decided to invest some of their substantial profit into new equipment for each area. The junior technicians in IT Support are to work as teams of three, with each team researching one of the following:

- an entertainment system for the public area
- a small business system for the offices
- a blade server for the network server room.

As the centre uses Dell as their preferred supplier, you have been asked to research the Dell website to evaluate suitable systems for your chosen area. (Make sure that all of these categories are covered across your class by at least one team.)

Go to the *www.dell.co.uk* website, then navigate to your team's choice of systems:

- entertainment system:
  Through *Desktops* then *Home* to press the *Choose Desktop* button in the *Desktop XPS & Performance* section
- small business system:
  Through *Desktops* then *Small Business* to press the *Choose Desktop* button in the *Dimension* section
- blade server:
  Through *Servers, Storage & Networking* then *Small Business* to press the *Choose Servers* button in the *Server Solutions* section.

Once you have reached the Dell web page showing your type of computer, use a *Customise* button for a suitable base model. What is the best balance you can find between performance and cost?

Task 1

Copy the best parts of your customised PC specification into a poster with the price and features that you included. Print a copy onto paper for each member of the team.

Task 2

As a class – or with a partner – discuss and agree how suitable three of the systems presented on the posters would be for their chosen area.

ACTIVITY 6

Go to your choice of websites to find compatible components:

- processor with fan
- motherboard
- RAM
- hard disk
- video connection using card or motherboard
- case with PSU
- keyboard and mouse
- display.

What is the cheapest customised system that you could build?

Copy the best parts of the specifications for your custom-built PC into a single page with 18 pt font size to summarise the price and features of your system. Print your summary out on A3 paper or onto clear plastic film to produce an overhead transparency (OHT) to be used with an overhead projector (OHP).

Your teacher/tutor will show the posters or OHTs to the rest of the group to highlight the price and features from each group. The class should give points to each system so that a 'best, cheap' system is found.

Useful websites will include:

www.ebuyer.co.uk

www.dabs.com

www.maplin.co.uk

www.pcworld.co.uk

www.smart-computers.net

ACTIVITY 7

You work as a junior analyst in the IT Services section of a large organisation with a wide variety of users.

One of the roles of IT Services is to decide what's on the preferred components list. The preferred components list is distributed to budget holders to help them price new systems and help plan future spending.

Use the Internet, computer magazines or a catalogue price list from a local computer shop to search hard-drive component specifications.

You then need to create this table:

	Cheapest	Fastest	Greatest capacity
Manufacturer			
Model			
Price (incl. VAT & carriage)			
Capacity			
Seek time			
Transfer rate			
Spin speed			

Complete your copy of the table with your choice of drives from the search. Which of these drives would you buy for your own system? Why?

Useful websites:

www.ebuyer.co.uk

www.dabs.com

www.maplin.co.uk

www.pcworld.co.uk

www.smart-computers.net

ACTIVITY 8

You work as a trainee applications programmer in a software house. The rest room has a two-year-old PC used by staff for gaming during their breaks. Jo, the managing director (MD), has offered to upgrade this PC and would like the team to decide what the replacement will be.

Your team leader has given everyone half an hour to specify the new PC.

Go to your choice of websites to find compatible components:

- processor with fan
- motherboard
- RAM
- hard disk
- video connection using card or motherboard
- case with PSU
- keyboard and mouse
- display.

What is the best gaming system that you can build? Why is this 'the best'? What does it cost?

Create a web page to show off the best parts of the specifications for your custom-built PC.

The team leader (your teacher/tutor) will show the web pages to the rest of the group to highlight the price and features from each. All of the teams should give points to each system to find the best gaming system.

Useful websites:

www.ebuyer.co.uk

www.dabs.com

www.maplin.co.uk

www.pcworld.co.uk

www.smart-computers.net

ACTIVITY 9

Another item on the preferred components list from the IT section in Activity 7 is video cards.

Use the Internet, computer magazines or a catalogue price list from a local computer shop to search video card component specifications for the AGP slot, then create the table overleaf.

Complete your copy of the table with your choice of video cards from the search. Which of these video cards would you buy for your own system? Why?

Useful websites:

www.ebuyer.co.uk

www.dabs.com

www.maplin.co.uk

www.pcworld.co.uk

www.smart-computers.net

	Cheapest	Fastest	Greatest capacity
Manufacturer			
Model			
Price (incl. VAT & carriage)			
Graphics processor			
Installed memory (MB)			
Memory type			
Clock speed (MHz)			

ACTIVITY 10

You trade on eBay in IT components and have a website advertising your current stock.

After receiving some questions about the operating speeds of different devices, you decide to add a page to your website with a bar chart showing the data transfer rates (DTR) of a variety of components and peripherals. The bar chart is to be in order, so the slowest component is at one end with the fastest at the other.

Include these devices using the fastest example of each that you can find:

- CD-ROM drive
- DVD drive
- external hard disk
- hard drive
- RAM
- USB pen drive.

Create a web page to display your bar chart.

ACTIVITY 11

The computer store where you work on the counter has received this email:

> Hi there,
>
> I'd like to purchase a cheap laptop (and whatever else is needed) so that I can connect to the Internet without plugging in cables. I already have broadband with BT which connects to my desktop PC using the USB port.
>
> Please can you answer these questions:
>
> 1) How far from the transmitter will I be able to use the laptop?
>
> 2) How fast is the transmission to the laptop?
>
> 3) How is the equipment set up?
>
> 4) What laptop do you recommend?
>
> Thanks,
>
> H. Smith

You need to produce a document that can be sent back as an attachment to answer these questions.

ACTIVITY 12

You build and sell computers in your spare time.

A customer has asked you how much you would charge for a maintenance contract.

Research these types of maintenance contract:

- return to base
- on-site
- next working day.

Produce a guide to each of these types of maintenance contract with a price for each that is in line with what you have seen in your research.

ACTIVITY 13

You work in the IT Services section of a large mail-order company.

The section produces a weekly newsletter that is circulated to all users with tips on how to use the computer systems, a guide to services offered to them and articles about IT products.

You have been asked to produce a series of articles, each explaining how to use a different input or output device. One of these articles will be printed each week in next month's departmental newsletter.

Produce two of these articles about different options.

SOFTWARE

ACTIVITY 14

You have been employed as a junior member of the helpdesk team for nearly a year.

A more senior position has become vacant in the section and you have decided to apply for this promotion. The interviewer has asked each applicant to give a short presentation explaining the purpose of an operating system. The interviewer wants to see the depth of each candidate's technical knowledge.

The presentation is to be on the purpose of operating system.

The purpose of an operating system is to provide an environment for the execution of programs by providing services needed by those programs.

The services programs request fall into five categories:

1   Process Control
2   File System Management
3   I/O Operation
4   Interprocess Communication
5   Information Maintenance.

The operating system must try to satisfy these requests in a multi-user, multi-process environment while managing:

- resource allocation
- error detection
- protection.

Use a search engine to search the *Images* pages with *operating system* as search phrase or find your own choice of website to choose some resources that you are able to understand and help you explain the purpose of a named operating system.

Use your chosen resources to create your interview presentation, showing the purpose of your named operating system.

Your tutor will select some presentations to be shown to the class and will then lead a question-and-answer session to check everyone's understanding.

Useful websites will include:

http://people.cs.uchicago.edu/~kaharris/cspp51081/Assignments/Assign2/lecture2.pdf

http://blogs.msdn.com/larryosterman/archive/2006/04/05/569099.aspx

http://www.codeplex.com/APOS

ACTIVITY 15

Operating systems have many features to tempt new users, such as being able to use a TV tuner to schedule the recording of TV programmes.

Your boss at the computer shop where you work wants a poster to explain to customers the benefits of some features included in the latest version of Windows, to help them decide whether to spend their money on an upgrade.

Look on-line to find four features that you find exciting in the Windows operating system.

Create a poster showing these features.

Useful websites:

http://www.sun.com/software/solaris/features.jsp

http://www.certiguide.com/apluso/cg_apo_
IIIOperatingSystemFeatures.htm
(Not Windows sites, but they do have useful general information)

http://www.wincustomize.com/articles.aspx?aid=66798&c=1

ACTIVITY 16

Your team leader has asked you to produce some pages for the company intranet for a new topic in the help pages explaining how company IT systems work.

The new topic is the functions of operating systems.

Operating systems have many functions including:

- machine and peripheral management
- security
- file management.

Look online to find out about each of these functions for a named operating system.

Useful websites:

http://www.comptechdoc.org/basic/basictut/osintro.html

http://www.bbc.co.uk/schools/gcsebitesize/ict/software/
4operatingsystemsrev2.shtml

http://www.webopedia.com/TERM/O/operating_system.html

Create a web page for the intranet that shows three functions of your named operating system, with hotspots linking to other pages explaining these hyperlinked topics from your main web page.

ACTIVITY 17

Select material from Activities 14–16 for two named operating systems such as Linux, MacOS or Windows, to cover their:

- purpose
- features
- functions.

Use this material to create a document with a table comparing them.

Activities 18–21 use a scenario of you working in a business that has based its IT systems on the Windows environment (although you may, of course, come across other systems in the business). In the activities, we imagine that you have all of the necessary access rights to the menu options discussed.

ACTIVITY 18

You work as a technician in the IT Support section of a legal practice. All of the solicitors who work from the practice have their own laptops that either have docking stations or WiFi to connect to the practice network.

There have been some helpdesk requests where work has been lost when working at home, so IT Support have decided to add pages to the user guide ring-binders in the practice, with guidance on how to back up data when away from the network.

'Backup' is a Windows software utility program used to copy data such as your work to CDR or another place. This keeps the data safe, so that if anything goes wrong with the computer, there is a back-up copy that can be restored. 'Restore' is an option in this utility to bring the backed-up data back from CDR or another place to where it came from on the hard disk.

You are to use this program to back-up some folders selected from your *My documents* onto a memory stick (or other media if you have them). Use Alt+PrtSc (*Print Screen*) to copy each page of selections you make using Backup and paste these into a Word document (Alt+PrtSc captures only the active window and not the desktop whereas PrtSc captures everything on screen).

Backup was installed into the *System tools* folder with other Windows utility programs.

To run the Backup program, use the Windows *Start* button then navigate *Programs, Accessories, System tools* to find *Backup*.

Backup has a wizard that first asks if you want to back-up or restore. This exercise asks you to back-up files from *My documents*, so the choice is *backup*.

The wizard asks what to back-up. Select the *Let me choose what to backup* option button on this screen. You can select a folder from the items-to-back-up window which the wizard will copy to your back-up media. Complete the back-up.

Use your screenshots to help create pages for the user guide showing how the Backup utility is used.

ACTIVITY 19

You work as a junior technician in the IT Support section of a large insurance company.

You have been asked to add pages to the 'procedures' ring-binder to guide other members of the team through some routine maintenance tasks for the company's computers.

'Disk cleanup' is a Windows software utility program used to clear unwanted files that have gathered on the hard disk. When a computer is used over a period of time old temporary files build up when the programs using them do not delete when completed. This occupies disk space unnecessarily.

You are to use this program to clear your disk space of unwanted files. Use Alt+PrtSc to copy each page of selections you make using Disk cleanup and paste these into a Word document as before.

Disk cleanup was installed into the *System tools* folder with other Windows utility programs. To run it, use the Windows *Start* button then navigate *Programs, Accessories, System tools* to find *Disk cleanup*.

Use this program to clear unwanted files that have gathered in your disk space and capture screenshots to help you complete activity tasks.

Create pages for the 'procedures' ring-binder from these screenshots showing how the Disk cleanup utility is used.

ACTIVITY 20

You have now been asked to add pages to the 'procedures' ring-binder to guide other members of the team through using 'Disk defragmenter'.

This is a Windows software utility program used to reorganise data on the hard disk. When a computer is used over a period of time, files get deleted and data on the disk gathers more and more 'gaps' in the way it's stored. This slows the computer system down as the hard disk read/write heads have to keep jumping around the disk to find the next empty place to save new work.

You are to use this program to defragment your disk space. Use Alt+PrtSc to copy each page of selections you make using Disk defragmenter and paste them into a Word document.

Disk defragmenter was installed into the *System tools* folder with other Windows utility programs. To run it, use the Windows *Start* button then navigate *Programs, Accessories, System tools* to find *Disk defragmenter.*

Use this program to defragment your disk space and capture screenshots to help you complete activity tasks.

Create pages for the 'procedures' ring-binder from these screenshots showing how the Disk defragmenter utility is used.

ACTIVITY 21

You have teamed up with a good friend to provide computer support and help for people who use their computers at home.

You both now realise that a lot of time can be wasted by visiting your clients when often problems can be solved over the telephone. Such calls are a lot more useful if the client has already got together some detailed information about their system.

So you decide to prepare a handout for clients explaining how to use the 'System information' utility to find out what's inside their systems.

System information is a Windows software utility program used to examine the many ways that the operating system connects hardware and software.

You are to find the following on your computer system using system information:

- DMA (hardware resources)
- IRQs (hardware resources)
- network adapter (components)
- printing (components)
- startup programs (software environment)
- Windows error reporting (software environment)
- system drivers (software environment).

Use Alt+PrtSc to copy each of these system information pages and paste into a Word document.

System information was installed into the *System tools* folder with other Windows utility programs. To run it, use the Windows *Start* button then navigate *Programs, Accessories, System tools* to find *System information*.

Use this program to look at the system information and capture a screenshot of each page you would find useful to help you support users.

Create a handout from your screenshots showing how System information utility is used.

ACTIVITY 22

Select material from Activities 18–21 for two named operating systems regarding:

- back-up
- disk clean-up
- disk defragmenter
- system information.

These resources will help you to explain how these software utility programs are used.

Create a document from your resources explaining how these software utility programs are used.

Your document should have a footer with your name and fields for file name, page number and print date. There should be a contents page created from heading styles.

ACTIVITY 23

The local library have heard that you have been doing well on your BTEC National Diploma course and have asked you to produce a display for the events notice board to show how operating systems for personal computers have evolved from the 1970s to the present day.

Create a time line of these operating systems – putting them into the proper order from oldest to newest – each with the release date and a comment about what each operating system brought to the market (why it will be remembered!):

- CP/M (Digital Research)
- PC-DOS 1.0 (IBM)
- Gem (Digital Research)
- MacOS 1.0 (Apple)
- MacOS X 1.0 (Apple)
- MS-DOS 6 (Microsoft)
- OS/2 (IBM)
- Windows 1.0 (Microsoft)
- Windows 3.1 (Microsoft)
- Windows 95 (Microsoft)
- Windows Vista (Microsoft)
- Windows XP (Microsoft)

ACTIVITY 24

You have a job with a computer consultancy as a junior analyst. The consultancy has been asked to brief the board of directors of a large local company about the security risks faced by operating systems and the features that are designed to secure the system.

Produce a presentation explaining how up to four security features in Windows Vista help to make it a more secure system than Windows XP.

ACTIVITY 25

You work as a junior technician in the IT Support section in the head office of a large supermarket chain.

Your line supervisor has sought permission from the board to replace the firewalls protecting the company systems, but his proposal was sent back with a request for more explanation of what a firewall actually does.

Produce a report explaining what a firewall is and how firewalls are used to protect computer systems.

COMPUTER MAINTENANCE

ACTIVITY 26

You work part-time for a superstore's regional office. The superstore has decided to mail a monthly booklet to customers showing special offers as well as tips and techniques on using computer systems.

Your line manager has been asked if anyone in their section can produce an article for the booklet called 'Why Defrag?'. You have now been given this job.

Select material from research regarding any documented effects that the disk defragmenter of a named operating system has on the performance of a computer system from the web or books.

These resources will help you to explain how disk defragmenter software maintenance affects the performance of a computer system.

Use your chosen resources to create an article explaining clearly how disk defragmenter software maintenance affects the performance of a computer system.

ACTIVITY 27

A virus checker is a program used to protect a computer system from viruses. As new viruses are being produced all the time, the virus protection should be updated with current data from the virus checker manufacturer's website.

On a visit to your grandparents you notice that their virus checker needs to be manually updated and so you do this for them. You try to explain how they can do that again next week, but it is quickly obvious that your words will be soon forgotten!

You decide to produce a simple guide to updating their virus checker for them.

Use a virus checker program to update from the manufacturer website. Use Alt+PrtSc to copy each page of selections you make using Disk cleanup, and paste into a Word document (Alt+PrtSc captures only the active window and not the desktop whereas PrtSc captures everything on screen).

Use your chosen resources to create a simple guide showing how to update the virus checker utility from the manufacturer's website.

ACTIVITY 28

You work as a freelance IT support technician with several clients. A lot of them are still unsure about how to keep Windows updated with the latest patches so you decide to produce a help sheet to explain how to do this.

A patch is a program update used to fix any problems found when people use the program. There are a lot of very active update pages on Microsoft websites for Windows to fix bugs and to address security issues discovered in versions of this operating system.

Start the Control panel then use Windows update to download and install any current patches available for your computer system. Use Alt+PrtSc to copy each page of selections you make using Disk cleanup, and paste into a Word document.

Use your chosen screenshots to create a help sheet showing how Windows update is used to download and install current patches available onto a computer system.

ACTIVITY 29

Some relatives are going on holiday soon and have asked your advice about how to send their photographs back to you from Australia. You suggest that they find an Internet café to log onto their emails then send the photos back as an attachment after compressing them into a zip file.

The relatives understand how to attach to emails, but don't know about compressing folders and files such as photographs.

Compressing a folder is used to prepare a folder for moving elsewhere as an email attachment, onto a pen drive or other media. Compressing reduces the size and brings the folder and contents into a single zip file.

Create a short document that they can take with them as a reminder of how to do this.

Select the folder to compress using a right click to bring up a menu, choose Send to, Compressed (zipped) folder. Follow the wizard to create a compressed copy of the folder you selected. Use Alt+PrtSc to copy each page of selections you make and paste them into a Word document.

Use your chosen screenshots to create step-by-step instructions showing how to create a compressed version of a folder.

ACTIVITY 30

Hands-on work needs safe working practices to protect yourself, others and the computer system components from harm and damage.

Safe working practices eliminate risk from electrical damage and sharp edges.

Electrical damage can be from static electricity that builds up on you, other people, surfaces and devices. Static electricity can damage the electronic circuits on components. Static electricity is removed by connecting to ground using anti-static wristbands and mats which must themselves connect to ground, using earth of mains electricity or an exposed metal surface on building pipe work. Electrical damage can also be from dangerous AC electricity that is provided by the mains and transformed down to a safe low DC voltage by the PSU (power supply unit). Danger is to yourself from mains AC electricity and to components from shorting out their low voltage connections. Both these dangers are removed when the system is unplugged from the mains. Components should only be removed when disconnected from mains.

There may be sharp edges in some cheaply produced cases. Be especially careful when pulling out cards or plugs and use a gentle, rocking action in preference to a lot of force!

In a table like this, record the safe working practices that you would use for each case of risk:

Name:_____ Date:_____

Risk	Prevention	What happened
Static electricity damaging component circuits		
Electrical danger from AC electricity to yourself		
Electrical danger from DC electricity to components		

ACTIVITY 31

Every printer that can be used by a computer has to be installed.

The computer shop where you work has asked you to add to their support pages on the website to help customers set up their printers.

Select *Printers and faxes* after using Windows *Start* button. Choose *Add printer* then follow the wizard to create a new printer object for a printer attached to the system. It is important that the correct printer is identified and confirmed working with a test print. Use Alt+PrtSc to copy each page of selections you make using the Add printer wizard and paste into a Word document.

Use your chosen screenshots to create a web page showing how to use the Add printer wizard with hotspots linking to other pages explaining parts of your web page.

ACTIVITY 32

You need to install a hard drive when a computer is built or as a hardware upgrade.

The owner of the computer shop where you work wants a rolling presentation to run on a computer in the shop to show technicians at work building PCs.

In reality, your first step would be to familiarise yourself with the health and safety rules of the hardware lab and follow them.

You might decide to use a digital still or video camera to record what you do.

Carefully take the cover off the PC, remove the existing hard disk and replace with a new disk. Make sure the red edge of ribbon cables are pointing to pin 1 on the sockets. Test the PC to confirm the hard disk is working correctly.

Copy the digital photographs or video onto your computer work space.

Use your chosen resources to create a presentation that can loop continuously that shows how to replace a hard disk. Make sure that the final slide can lead onto the first so that the show looks seamless when running in the shop.

ACTIVITY 33

You work as a junior technician in the IT Support section of a large call centre.

The call centre has a workbench where broken computers and peripherals are taken apart and repaired. Unfortunately, there have been some recent accidents when repairing computers and damage to components from static electricity.

Create a poster explaining good, safe working practices for repairing IT equipment. The poster will be displayed on the wall behind the workbench.

ACTIVITY 34

You might often need to install a graphics card when a computer has a hardware upgrade to help it run gaming software. Graphics cards are also known as video cards.

The owner of the computer shop where you work has already asked you to produce a rolling presentation to run on a computer in the shop to show technicians at work building PCs. This has been well received and now a new section is to be added showing a graphics card being installed.

Again, in a real situation, you would need to familiarise yourself with the health and safety rules of the hardware lab and follow them.

You may use a digital still or video camera to record what you do.

Carefully take the cover off the PC, remove the existing graphics card and replace it with a new one. Test the PC to confirm that the display is working correctly.

Copy the digital photographs or video onto your computer work space.

Create pages for a presentation showing how to upgrade a graphics card which can loop continuously. Make sure the last slide can lead onto the first so that the show looks seamless when running in the shop.

ACTIVITY 35

The computer shop where you work has asked you to produce a short guide to upgrading these components in a computer system:

- printer
- hard drive
- video card.

Use on-line resources to research components for each of these upgrades. These resources will help you decide which parts of the specifications can be used to explain how to select components for upgrades of a computer system.

Create a document explaining what to look for when selecting components for upgrades of a computer system as a short guide.

ACTIVITY 36

A old friend asked you to look at their computer as it is running very, very slowly.

You found that it could barely boot up (probably because of a virus problem) and decide to re-install the operating system.

After re-installing the operating system and application software, your friend asks how to avoid problems from spyware and other on-line threats in the future. You start to explain, but it is quickly clear that your friend does not understand so you decide to produce a short document – with pictures – to explain how spyware operates and how to minimise the risks in the future.

This is the document that you need to create for this activity.

ACTIVITY 37

You have become quite successful providing home computer support to many of the people in the area. To improve the support you offer and to publicise your services, you have been working on a website providing support advice and a discussion forum.

You have now decided to add a page to the site linking to other websites that offer drivers for download for a wide variety of computer components.

Produce a web page with a screenshot of each of six websites offering drivers for download. These screenshot images should each link to their website, so that clicking on a screenshot will bring up that site.

This section focuses on grading criteria P1, P5; M1 and D1 from Unit 3 – Information Systems.

Learning outcomes

1 Know the source and characteristics of business information.

3 Understand the issues and constraints in relation to the use of information in organisations.

Content

1) Know the source and characteristics of business information

Characteristics: distinction between data and information; type of information (qualitative, quantitative); primary; secondary; characteristics of good information, eg valid, reliable, timely, fit-for-purpose, accessible, cost-effective, sufficiently accurate, relevant, having the right level of detail, from a source in which the user has confidence, understandable by the user; transformation of data into information (collection, storage, processing and manipulation, retrieval, presentation).

Sources of information: internal, eg financial, personnel, marketing, purchasing, sales, manufacturing, administration; external, eg government, trade groupings, commercially provided, databases, research; reliability of data sources.

3) Understand the issues and constraints in relation to the use of information in organisations

Legal issues: relevant data protection legislation, eg Data Protection Act 1998, Freedom of Information Act 2000; other relevant legislation, eg Computer Misuse Act 1990.

Ethical issues: codes of practice, eg on use of email, Internet, 'whistle blowing'; organisational policies; information ownership.

Operational issues: security of information; backups; health and safety; organisational policies; business continuance plans; costs, eg additional resources required,

cost of development; impact of increasing sophistication of systems, eg more trained personnel, more complex software.

Grading criteria

P1 describe the characteristics and sources of information that an organisation needs

This will require you to have an understanding of where businesses can find information to meet their business needs, what it should look like and how useful it will be to them.

P5 identify the constraints that relate to the use of customer information in an organisation and describe how these may impact on the organisation

This asks you to think about what might restrict the use of particular information in a business and how these restrictions might affect the way in which the business can run.

In order to meet this criterion you will need to investigate different acts of parliament and laws and be able to decide the impact that these might have on organisations' functions. You will also discuss different ethical problems and operational issues that could affect the workplace and the systems developed within it. You will also need to know how an organisation can influence internal policies when using information systems. The best way to tackle this aspect is to try and see what would be needed in such a policy and then think about the restrictions that this could have in a business.

M1 explain the importance to an organisation of effectively collecting, processing and using information

This will expect you to be able to talk about the reasons behind the best ways of finding, transforming and making use of information in a business environment. As far as the first learning outcome is concerned you will only be looking at the areas where any business could possibly look for relevant and appropriate information.

D1 explain how an organisation could improve the quality of its business information, justifying each of their recommendations

This requires that you can make decisions, and prove your reasons for these decisions, showing how any business can find and make use of information. As far as the first learning outcome is concerned you will be examining the best ways to get the most relevant information and giving your reasons for the ways identified.

In order to meet the first learning outcome you will need to understand the difference between data and information and how one makes the other. You will also need to gain an ability to evaluate different sources and characteristics of information and how to use information effectively in given circumstances.

The activities throughout this section of the book will lead you towards the knowledge and understanding to be able to achieve this criterion and any higher grade criteria.

CHARACTERISTICS OF BUSINESS INFORMATION

ACTIVITY 1

There is a difference between data and information. Data must be processed before it can become information. Data can be collected from a wide range of sources. Data can be transformed into different information dependent on the need. Information can be used for a variety of purposes. In the case of information developed from information systems, many of the purposes are management-based.

Individually, draw a simple diagram to represent the definition that 'Information is data processed for a purpose'.

ACTIVITY 2

Secondary data are data that have already been collected by someone else for a different purpose to yours. For example, this could mean using:

■ data collected by a hotel on its customers through its guest history system

■ data supplied by a marketing organisation

■ annual company reports

■ government statistics.

Primary data collection is necessary when the data needed cannot be found in secondary sources. Three basic means of obtaining primary data are:

■ observation

■ surveys

■ experiments.

All methods of data collection can supply quantitative data (numbers, statistics or financial) or qualitative data (usually words or text). Quantitative data may often be presented in tabular or graphical form.

Task 1

In small groups, consider how you might collect primary data when setting-up a new information system in your college. Discuss what sort of data might be collected. Think about whether it would be quantitative or qualitative or both. Decide to what purpose this data might be put. Would you need to use all three possible methods? What other methods might you use? Add to a copy of the table below; add extra rows if required. Report the group findings back to the class.

Method of collecting the data	Type of data (qualitative, quantitative, or both)	Purpose (what the data will be used for)
Observation		
Survey		
Experiment		

Task 2

In small groups, consider any secondary data that your college might need to examine when comparing its performance against its competitors. Identify possible sources and reasons for use of the secondary data. Decide whether the data might be quantitative or qualitative or both. Report the group findings back to the class.

Source of the data (where it came from)	Data collected (what it was)	Type of data (qualitative, quantitative or both)	Purpose (what the data will be used for)

Task 3

Transformation means performing some change on data in this situation. You may alter the data slightly or put it into a different format or put it into some more meaningful structure. From the two previous tasks and in the same small groups, examine how the raw data collected could be transformed into information that is more meaningful and can be understood more quickly. Some of this work might involve processing the data. Other data transformations might just involve changing the structure of how the data is laid out. You need to consider:

Transformation method (how the data is collected)	Transformation outcome (what the result could be)
Collection	
Storage	
Processing	
Manipulation	
Retrieval	
Presentation	

Task 4

In the same small groups, imagine that you are setting up a new small business. The business concerned is called BITs4U. Its aim is to provide sales of specialist computer parts to customers. Once the parts are supplied, the owner offers an installation service for those customers not willing to do the work themselves. It is being set up because the owner has been doing some work already for a small group of friends and believes he can make a living from this work. The owner needs to begin to put together a business plan to present to the bank manger in his quest for start-up funds.

What information would you seek, where would you look for it, what sort of information would it be (qualitative, quantitative or both)? Write a group report, using similar tabular structures as used in Tasks 1 to 3, to help the owner put his plan together. Save this report, as you will need it in later activities.

ACTIVITY 3

Information is no good to the user unless it has certain characteristics that make it fit for purpose. Information is usually classified as having the following properties or characteristics:

Valid	Is it suitable and applicable?
Reliable	Is it dependable and consistent?
Timely	Has it come at the right time and is it sensible?
Accessible	Is it easily available?
Cost-effective	Has the collection avoided undue expense and time?
Sufficiently accurate	Can enough reliance be placed on it?
Relevant	Is it appropriate in the situation?
Having the right level of detail	Does it provide enough facts and figures for the business or user to make good use of it? This is usually linked with Accuracy and Relevance.
From a source in which the user has confidence	Is it a trustworthy link, text or document? Does the user feel comfortable with it? This is usually linked with Valid and Reliable.
Understandable by the user	Does the reader know what it means? Perhaps it could be 'transformed' into something more useful? Is it accessible?
Fit for purpose	Will it do the job for which it was collected?

Each of the aspects below needs to be considered as well (if there any words here that you do not understand you should use a dictionary to find the meaning before you go any further):

- how to identify information which may be contradictory, ambiguous or inadequate and how to deal with these problems
- the importance of information management to the team and organisational effectiveness and the user's role and responsibilities in relation to this
- the types of qualitative and quantitative information which are essential to the user's role and responsibilities, and how to identify these
- the range of sources of information that are available to users and how to ensure that these are capable of meeting current and likely future information requirements
- how to identify new sources of information which may be required
- the range of methods of gathering and checking the validity of such information and their advantages and disadvantages
- the organisational values and policies and the legal requirements which have a bearing on the collection of information and how to interpret these.

Task 1

Read the list above and, in small groups, complete a copy of the table below on why each aspect should be met and how you could achieve it. Discuss your answers with the rest of the class.

Description of your data	Why it is important that your data is like this	How to make sure that your data is like this
Valid		
Reliable		
Timely		
Accessible		
Cost-effective		
Sufficiently accurate		
Relevant		
Having the right level of detail		
From a source in which the user has confidence		
Understandable by the user		

Task 2

Following on from the previous task, draw up a generic set of criteria that you would apply to any piece of information each time you read it. Do this as a class activity so that all of you are taking the same approach. Identify four or five major criteria from the list you develop. List them in a table.

Task 3

Using your ideas from Task 4 for BITs4U (Activity 2) and working in the same small groups, justify your choices of information sources against the generic criteria developed in Task 2. Add to your earlier report and save it for future use.

82

SOURCES OF BUSINESS INFORMATION

ACTIVITY 4

Information comes from two areas for any organisation:

- internal to the company
- external to the company.

Internal means that various departments within the company produce figures, reports, etc, which management will use to make decisions about the way in which the company can do business.

External means that information is gleaned from other areas that might influence the way in which a company does business.

You have already looked at some methods of data collection of both primary and secondary data sources. You have also already decided whether particular types of data are qualitative or quantitative. Another aspect you have addressed is transforming the data into the most meaningful format for the user.

Task 1

In small groups, complete a copy of the following table identifying potential information that could come from each of the departments listed. Think about other functions in an organisation that might produce information, and add them to the list.

Department	Outputs
Accounts	
Administration	
Distribution	
Personnel	
Purchasing	
Sales	

Task 2

You have already looked at different sources of external information and the purpose to which each might be put. Using the following case study, consider different external sources of information the hotel might consult in order to drive its business forward. Decide, again, whether it would be qualitative, quantitative or both. Think about why the hotel would need the information.

> This hotel in Manchester is ideal for accommodation in Manchester as well as being a Manchester hotel conference venue. This Manchester hotel has facilities available for family holidays, countryside, City, adventure, walking, activity holidays, long, short, or weekend breaks for shopping or attraction visiting, engagements, birthdays, christenings, retirement, Civil Services, wedding receptions, fine dining, entertainment, function, special events, celebration, business and corporate accommodation, conference services and training facilities, even working lunches. For a cheap hotel in Manchester with great value for money try the Monton House Hotel Manchester. This Manchester Hotel is superbly placed for visitors to The Trafford Centre, Manchester United Football Club, Old Trafford Cricket Club, Salford Quays, The Lowry, The Imperial War Museum, Manchester City Centre, Daytona Go-carting, The Palace Theatre, The Apollo Theatre and many more attractions (http://www.montonhousehotel.co.uk/).

Source of the data (where it came from)	Data collected (what it was)	Type of data (qualitative, quantitative or both)	Purpose (what the data will be used for)

Task 3

The government publishes figures about people coming to the UK. To what use could the hotel put information like this?

> In the three months to March 2007 there were 8.5 million visits to the UK by overseas residents, an increase of 2 per cent when compared with the previous three months, while the associated spending decreased to £3.7 billion. (http://www.statistics.gov.uk/cci/nugget.asp?id=352)

Task 4

Using the criteria that you created in Activity 3, Task 2 and the sources you found in Task 3, have a class discussion on the fitness-for-purpose of those sources.

Task 5

Using your ideas from Task 4 for BITs4U (Activity 2) and working in the same small groups, decide what internal information might you need as the business starts to operate? Add to your earlier report from Activity 3, Task 3 and save it for future use with later activities.

ACTIVITY 5

To consolidate the theory from the first learning outcome you should carry out a real data-collection activity.

Task 1

Go to URL http://www.statistics.gov.uk/census/pdfs/2007_test_H1_form.pdf and download a copy of the census test form. In small groups, create a similar census for use in your school or college. You can ignore some of the questions as they will not be important. You may choose to add some extra questions.

Task 2

Use this census and interview your year group in school or college. Collate the results that you have found, using of course only matching questions otherwise the information could be deemed meaningless.

Task 3

Compare your findings with those from the most recent census taken nationally. Decide whether there are any deviations or differences and evaluate why these might be.

Task 4

In small groups, discuss who could make use of the data you collated and what information they could draw from it. Decide whether the information, when used, is quantitative or qualitative, primary or secondary. Feed your ideas back to the rest of the class.

Task 5

Discuss, in class, the techniques you used to transform the data into meaningful information. Think about the characteristics of the information you have produced. What could you have done differently to produce the information from your collected data? Would other people think your sources are reliable?

LEGAL ISSUES

ACTIVITY 6

In the UK, laws and acts of Parliament are in place to ensure that, wherever possible, people's rights are preserved.

Task 1

Use the Internet to find out about the **Freedom of Information Act 2000** and write a brief report (100 words) describing the main features of the act.

Task 2

Use the Internet to find out about the **Data Protection Act 1998** and write a brief report (100 words) describing the main features of the act.

Task 3

Use the Internet to find out about the **The Computer Misuse Act 1990** and write a brief report (100 words) describing the main features of the act.

Task 4

Use the Internet to find out about the **The Privacy and Electronic Communications Regulations 2003** and write a brief report (100 words) describing the main features of the regulations.

Task 5

Now that you have an understanding of various legal aspects that can affect work environments consider, in small groups, how these might affect the development of information systems and organisations that use them. Report your findings to the whole class.

Task 6

Building on your ideas, BITs4U now wants to start putting together an organisational policy that any new employee would be obliged to follow. Show how these legal implications could affect the running of the organisation. Develop a new report for the policy and save the report for future use. You should undertake this task in the same small groups you were in for previous activities relating to BITs4U.

ETHICAL ISSUES

ACTIVITY 7

There are several ethical issues that are involved in the use of information systems. Many of these issues are now being incorporated into organisational policies for the operation of systems. These issues include appropriate use of email, whistle blowing and information ownership.

Consider the following code taken from the Internet:

> The Code aims to:
>
> - encourage employees to feel confident in raising serious concerns and to question and act upon their concerns
>
> - provide ways for employees to raise those concerns and get feedback on any action taken as a result
>
> - ensure that employees get a response to their concerns and that they are aware of how to pursue them, and if they know what to do if they are not satisfied with any responses
>
> - reassure employees that if they raise any concerns in good faith and reasonably believe them to be true, they will be protected from possible reprisals or victimisation.
>
> (http://www.birmingham.gov.uk/GenerateContent?CONTENT_ITEM_ID=10821&CONTENT_ITEM_TYPE=0&MENU_ID=11168&EXPAND=10838)

Task 1

Discuss, in small groups, the implications of such a code of practice. Consider how it could be incorporated into an organisational policy for the use of information systems. Feed your ideas back to the whole class and highlight the key common thoughts.

Task 2

Back with the BITs4U groups, discuss whether any such code of practice would be effective in the small organisation. What would happen if business expanded greatly and the employee base grew from a handful to over 50? Would this be more beneficial?

Organisational policies will require some code of practice, even in a small company like BITs4U. Add a couple of extra points, from your discussions, to your policy developed in Activity 6, Task 6.

ACTIVITY 8

Email etiquette is becoming an important aspect considered by many organisations these days.

Task 1

Individually, examine the content found at the URL http://www.lse.ac.uk/itservices/Rules/email.htm and highlight two aspects of good practice and two of bad practice that you think are the most important.

Task 2

Discuss, in class, how you think you behave when using email. Do you follow good practice? How can you ensure that your colleagues in a work environment obey guidelines on the use of email?

Task 3

Back with the BITs4U groups, discuss whether any email etiquette should be applied in the small organisation. Again, what would happen if business expanded greatly and the employee base grew from a handful to over 50; would this then be more beneficial?

Organisational policies will require some email etiquette aspects, even in a small company like BITs4U. Add a couple of extra points, from your discussions, to your policy developed in Activity 7, Task 2.

ACTIVITY 9

Information ownership means every document, data file or web page has to be owned by a nominated person. They are responsible for:

- the accuracy and currency of the information provided
- ensuring that, if the information has come from another source, the source is clearly identified
- providing the name (or job title/team name) along with an email address (or preferably an online form) and a telephone number to whom a visitor can address any queries.

This standard is of particular importance because information suppliers are legally responsible for the accuracy of their data since the Data Protection Act 1984.

Task 1

Discuss, in class, how you think this can be enforced. What would you need to do to ensure every employee is aware of their responsibilities?

Task 2

Back with the BITs4U groups, discuss, building on your discussions from the previous task, how information ownership could be enforced. Would it be necessary? Write up your discussions as an expansion to the developmental organisational policy and save for future use by extending the report from Activity 8, Task 3.

Organisational policies will require some information ownership aspects, even in a small company like BITs4U. Add a couple of extra points, from your discussions, to your policy developed in Activity 8, Task 3.

OPERATIONAL ISSUES

There are many internal factors that can cause problems or create required changes in the way in which a business operates when an organisation sets up an information system. Some of these issues are:

- making sure the data stored is safe and secure from 'intruders'
- ensuring there is a back-up strategy in place in case of hardware failure
- following health and safety guidelines on the use of computer systems
- in stating a policy for the use of hardware and software
- struggling with increasingly complex software systems
- making sure that all staff are able to use the system
- ensuring there is a replacement and upgrade strategy in place
- ensuring there are sufficient funds in place
  - to buy the extra equipment and resources
  - to allow for the development programme.

In order to deal with these aspects many organisations set up a policy that all employees must follow. In fact, many of the previous tasks have led you to develop such a policy.

ACTIVITY 10

Task 1

In small groups, investigate current methods, hardware and software, that could be used to protect data stored on a computer. Feed your findings back to the class, noting the key features.

Task 2

In class, discuss the different approaches to creating a back-up strategy – this could be both hardware and software. Note the key features.

Task 3

Back with the BITs4U groups, discuss back-up approaches that BITs4U could adopt.

Organisational policies will require some system back-up aspects, even in a small company like BITs4U. Add a couple of extra points, from your discussions, to your policy developed in Activity 8, Task 3.

HEALTH AND SAFETY AT WORK

All workers have a right to work in places where risks to their health and safety are properly controlled. The primary responsibility for this is down to the employer. Workers have a right to join and be represented by a trade union. Both workers and employers have a legal responsibility to look after health and safety at work together. Workers who contribute to health and safety at work are safer – and possibly healthier – than those who do not.

In the Unit 1 section of this Study Guide, you were asked to undertake activities relating to health and safety. If you did not do them then, do them now. If you did do them, then revisit what you found out.

ACTIVITY 11

Task 1

In class, identify the key features of **health and safety** that should be included in an organisational policy.

Task 2

Which aspects from the previous task could have an effect on the development and use of an information system? – be selective and thoughtful.

Task 3

Back with the BITs4U groups, discuss health and safety approaches that BITs4U could adopt.

Organisational policies will require some health and safety aspects, even in a small company like BITs4U. Add a couple of extra points, from your previous discussions, to your policy developed in Activity 10, Task 3.

REPORTS AND POLICIES

ACTIVITY 12

Task 1

In Activity 6 you looked at various other legal requirements. From these, in small groups, pull together some key features that could affect organisations and the development of a common policy for operations. Feed your findings back to the class, noting the common key features identified by each small group.

Task 2

Ask your school/college computer technician to check your ideas and see which are currently in operation within your school/college.

Task 3

Back with the BITs4U groups, using the report outcome from Activity 11, put your ideas together into a prototype organisational policy for the small business.

ACTIVITY 13

In the activities for Unit 1 you considered different ways of identifying training needs. When introducing new information systems or operating existing ones, staff need to be capable of operating these securely and appropriately.

Task 1

In class discussions, consider why and when training might be necessary. Identify when it should be undertaken and by whom. Create some key aspects that could be considered for inclusion in an organisational policy.

Task 2

Again, in BITs4U groups, discuss training needs and how these might be put into effect in a small business. Would the owner be expecting to employ only trained, experienced staff? Would the owner be happy to take on school leavers with little knowledge and understanding of the business and its structure or its installation activities?

Organisational policies will require some training and development aspects, even in a small company like BITs4U. Add a couple of extra points, from your discussions, to your policy developed in Activity 11, Task 3.

ACTIVITY 14

Task 1

Now you have gathered ideas for an organisational policy that could affect information systems operations within an organisation, talk to your school/college computer technician and check your ideas to see which are currently in operation within your school/college. Ask the technician about the policy on replacement and upgrade of equipment.

Task 2

Again, in BITs4U groups, is there anything about replacement and upgrade issues that could affect the small business? If so, extend your policy (from Activity 13, Task 2) to incorporate your ideas.

ACTIVITY 15

Now that you have carefully put together a prototype organisational policy based on your discussions about aspects such as those in the content for this area (security of information; back-ups; health and safety; organisational policies; business continuance plans; costs, eg additional resources required, cost of development; impact of increasing sophistication of systems, eg more trained personnel, more complex software) you should consider how the constraints therein could affect the use of information.

Task 1

Complete a copy of the table with each of the points from your policy:

Aspect/point from prototype policy	Relevance to BITs4U – is it important? – will it affect the way in which the company operates?	Relevance to customer information held in any information system – is it important at this stage?	Constraints on the use of customer information – will it have any effect on the use by any organisation of information held about customers? If so, what? Could it be a help or a hindrance?

Add extra rows if your prototype policy is larger than expected!

UNIT 15 – ORGANISATIONAL SYSTEMS SECURITY

This section focuses on grading criteria P1, P2, P3, P4, P5, P6, P7; M1, M2, M3 and aspects of D1 and D2 from Unit 15 – Organisational Systems Security.

Learning outcomes

1 Know potential threats to ICT systems and organisations.

2 Understand how to keep systems and data secure.

3 Understand the organisational issues affecting the use of ICT systems.

Content

1) Know potential threats to ICT systems and organisations

Unauthorised access: internal and external; access causing damage to data or jamming resources, eg viruses; accessing systems or data without damage; specific examples, eg phishing, identity theft, piggybacking, hacking.

Damage to or destruction of systems or information: natural disasters; malicious damage (internal and external causes); technical failures; human errors; theft.

Information security: confidentiality; integrity and completeness of data; availability of data as needed.

Threats related to e-commerce: website defacement; control of access to data via third party suppliers; other, eg denial of service attacks.

Counterfeit goods: products at risk, eg software, DVDs, games, music; distribution mechanisms, eg boot sales, peer-to-peer networks.

Organisational impact: loss of service; loss of business or income, eg through loss of customer records; increased costs; poor image.

2) Understand how to keep systems and data secure

Physical security: locks; visitor's passes; sign in/out systems; others, eg guards, cable shielding.

Biometrics: retinal scans; fingerprint; other, eg voice recognition.

Software and network security: encryption techniques, eg public and private key; call back; handshaking; diskless networks; use of backups; audit logs; firewall configuration; virus-checking software; use of virtual private networks (VPN); intruder detection systems; passwords; levels of access to data; software updating.

3) Understand the organisational issues affecting the use of ICT systems

Security policies and guidelines: disaster-recovery policies; updating of security procedures and scheduling of security audits; codes of conduct, eg email usage policy, Internet usage policy, software acquisition and installation policy; surveillance and monitoring policies; risk management; budget setting.

Employment contracts and security: hiring policies; separation of duties; ensuring compliance including disciplinary procedures; training and communicating with staff as to their responsibilities.

Code of conduct: email usage policy; Internet usage policy; software acquisition and installation policy; user area usage policy; account management policy.

Laws: eg Computer Misuse Act 1990; Copyright, Designs and Patents Act 1988; Privacy and compensation requirements of Data Protection Act 1984, 1998, 2000.

Copyrights: open source; freeware; shareware; commercial software.

Ethical decision making: eg freedom of information versus personal privacy (electoral roll, phone book and street maps put together); permission, eg to use photographs or videos, CCTV footage.

Professional bodies: eg Business Software Alliance (BSA), Federation Against Software Theft (FAST), British Computing Society (BCS), Association of Computing Machinery (ACM).

Grading criteria

P1 describe the various types of threats to organisations, systems and data

This means you will need to provide a description of all the security threats that can affect an organisation, computer systems and the data held on the systems.

P2 describe the potential impact of four different threats

This means you will need to, for four of the threats described in P1, give an account of the possible results if they actually occurred.

P3 describe the countermeasures available to an organisation that will reduce the risk of damage to information

This means that you should give an account of all the different ways that computer systems can be protected from damage occurring to the data and information held on them. 'Damage' means things like the data being erased or altered.

P4 describe the countermeasures available to an organisation that will reduce the risk of damage to physical systems

This means that you should give an account of all the different ways that an organisation can reduce the likelihood that computer systems will be physically damaged.

P5 describe different methods of recovering from a disaster

This means that you should give an account of all the different ways that an organisation can recover its data and computer systems from a disaster (such as a fire or flood).

P6 describe the tools and policies an organisation can adopt in managing organisational issues in relation to ICT security

This means that you should list the various tools and policies that an organisation may adopt, but must then go on to detail the characteristics of each of them as they relate to the organisation's issues around ICT security. A list on its own is not enough! Link the descriptions to the legislation in this area to show that you understand the reasons behind that legislation. You have to show that ICT security policy is not just about catching criminals, but also about allowing an organisation to employ the right staff and then to train them in acceptable use of the organisation's IT equipment.

P7 describe how staff contracts and code of conduct can assist the task of ensuring secure systems

This means you should state how contracts of employment and employee codes of conduct should include rules or guidelines about using computer systems that help keep an organisation's computer systems secure.

M1 explain possible security issues which exist within a given system

This means you will need to make clear all the security issues which may affect a particular computer system. The particular system you are explaining the threats for will need to be defined either by you or your tutor.

M2 explain the operation and effect of two different threats involving gaining access to information without damage to data

This means you will need to take two threats which involve how information can be accessed but not damaged and make clear how the threat actually works and the possible effects that it may have.

M3 explain the operation and use of an encryption technique in ensuring security of transmitted information

This means that you should make clear how one encryption technique (such as public/private key) works and how it can be used to transmit data over a network.

D1 describe the possible security issues which exist within a given system, identifying the likelihood of each and propose acceptable steps to counter the issues

This means you will need to give an account of the security issues which may affect a particular computer system and for each one you should say how likely it is that the issue will affect the system. You also need to say what you would do to protect the system from each security issue.

D2 justify the security policies used in an organisation

This requires you to assess what is acceptable behaviour in today's IT industry and to link that to security policies to enforce that behaviour. Acceptable behaviour can be taken to be what is recommended by the various lead professional bodies operating in the industry; you will need to show that you have evaluated the usefulness of lead professional bodies, ie formed your own impressions of them and shown how they impact on the security policies in use in the IT industry.

THREATS TO SYSTEMS

ACTIVITY 1

The topic of IT system security is full of technical terms, which describe the types of attacks that can occur. It is important to know the terms and their meanings, so creating a computer security glossary for yourself is a worthwhile process. The following list shows some of the more common terms (but new terms come into use all the time, so you may be able to add more to the list). Find definitions for each of these terms.

- Adware
- Blackhat
- Botnet
- Denial of service
- Drive-by download
- Exploit
- Keylogger
- Malware
- Packet sniffing
- Phishing
- Piggybacking
- Spyware
- Trojan
- Whitehat
- Worm
- Zero-day attack
- Zombie

ACTIVITY 2

Purchasing counterfeit goods such as DVDs, games and software has the obvious benefit of low cost, but there are a number of drawbacks as well. Make a list of the possible drawbacks. You should consider not just how purchasing these goods may adversely affect you but the possible consequences for others (eg manufacturers) and society as a whole.

Have a small group discussion or debate on the subject of counterfeit goods. If you have a debate the motion could be: 'This house believes that purchasing counterfeit goods is selfish and irresponsible'.

ACTIVITY 3

In small groups, discuss the following questions:

- Organisations that are victims of 'Cyber Crime' rarely publicise the fact that they have suffered such attacks. Why is this? What affect does this lack of publicity have on the general public and on those who might be considering such an attack?

- When Microsoft Windows Vista was launched, claims were made that is was the safest version of Windows ever. Why might it be unwise to make claims about how secure a piece of software or a system is?

- Windows XP is infamous for the number of security loopholes which have been found. Has Vista suffered from any serious security loopholes?

- Why have so many more security loopholes been found in Windows operating systems as opposed to Linux?

ACTIVITY 4

Task 1

Phishing attacks are very common at the moment. What is a phishing attack? Who does it affect and how does it work? Internet browsers such as Microsoft Internet Explorer (Version 7) and Morzilla Firefox have anti-phishing filters. How do these work?

Task 2

Create a poster or leaflet to warn computer users of the dangers of phishing attacks and give advice on how to avoid them.

ACTIVITY 5

Task 1

In late 2005 Swedish Bank Nordea lost about £500 000 in what was at the time one of the largest on-line frauds ever. Research into how the fraud was carried out and create a short list of the things that the fraudsters did. (You can start by searching for 'Nordea' on the BBC news website – www.bbc.co.uk/news – or by searching using Google). How could the bank's customers have protected themselves from the fraud?

Task 2

Have any other big Internet or computer scams or frauds occurred recently? (Again, the BBC website is a good place to start searching.)

ACTIVITY 6

Task 1

Computer systems which include wireless access are vulnerable to a number of threats that don't affect wired networks.

Make a list of the ways in which wireless networks can be misused by hackers. For each vulnerability, say how the network can be protected.

Task 2

Create a simple guide for home PC users (in the form of a poster or web page) that explains the dangers of wireless networks and how to protect against them.

KEEPING SYSTEMS AND DATA SECURE

ACTIVITY 7

So-called 'zero-day' attacks are of particular concern since traditional protection methods are ineffective. What is a 'zero-day' attack? Research the methods that can be used to provide protection against these types of attack.

Create a leaflet or poster that warns users of the dangers of zero-day attacks and gives advice on how to try to protect themselves against them.

How might a user's choice of operating system be influenced by the danger of zero-day attacks? What advice would you give a user on operating system choice in relation to security?

ACTIVITY 8

Passwords are the most commonly used form of computer security, and PIN codes are a type of password that are also widely used (mobile phones, credit and debit cards, etc).

Discuss in small groups what the advantages and disadvantages of password and PIN code are. Can you think of ways of reducing these disadvantages? What recommendations would you make to people about creating secure but easy-to-use passwords?

ACTIVITY 9

Biometrics is a science that is still in its infancy, but many people believe that it will play an important role in the future of computer security. Some biometric authentication systems are already in use while others are still being developed.

Research the various methods that biometric authentication can use and find out how effective each one is. Find out what are the benefits and possible drawbacks of biometric authentication. Create a table listing all the different techniques, describing how they work, how effective (accurate) they are and what their benefits and drawbacks are.

ACTIVITY 10

Research the following questions related to virtual private networks (VPNs):

- What is a virtual private network (VPN)?
- What are the benefits of a VPN over other forms of network?
- Why is security a big issue with VPNs?
- What methods can be used to secure VPNs?

ACTIVITY 11

Discuss the following questions in small groups:

- What are the basic requirements for sending coded (encrypted) messages?
- Can you think of a way you could create an encryption scheme for sending coded emails or text messages?
- How difficult would your scheme be to crack?
- Simple encryption schemes such as transposing letters of the alphabet are generally quite easy to crack. What techniques can be used to crack them? (tip: read the article on encryption in Wikipedia)

ACTIVITY 12

Computing is at the heart of the science of cryptography; the very first computers built during World War II were used to decrypt enemy messages. However, cryptography is much older than that and is also related to mathematics. Cryptography is also a highly complex science and in recent years has become the subject of a great deal of study and controversy.

What purposes is encryption put to in computer security?

Microsoft Windows Vista includes a feature (on some versions) called BitLocker. What is this feature for and how does it work?

Encryption is also important in digital rights management (DRM) systems, which are used to prevent copyright digital material, such as music or video files, from being copied. What DRM techniques are currently used? How do they work (from both a technical point of view and a user point of view)? What restrictions do they place on the use of the media?

ACTIVITY 13

A firewall is an important tool to protect computers that are attached to the Internet. Research the answers to these questions:

- What is a firewall and how does it work?
- What different types of firewalls are there and how do they differ from each other?
- Windows XP and Vista include a personal firewall. Create a simple guide for a novice IT user which explains the purpose of the firewall and how to configure and use it.
- Another well-known personal firewall is Zone Alarm (produced by Check Point Software). How does it differ from the firewall included in Windows?
- What is a proxy server? How can one be used to protect a computer system and to enforce Internet usage rules?

ACTIVITY 14

Software security systems to protect people from threats from hackers, viruses, etc, tend to be the main topics for computer security people to think about, but physical security is also important. These include systems to control entry to buildings and track location of employees and visitors within a building, as well and mechanisms to prevent the physical removal of computer hardware.

Task 1

What access control and physical security mechanisms do you use at your school or college (if any)? In small groups, discuss their purpose and effectiveness.

Research the market for both access control equipment and physical security (lock, etc) for computer systems. Based on your research, recommend equipment that could be used to improve the physical security in your school or college.

Task 2

There have been several high-profile cases recently where laptops containing sensitive information such as customer or banking details or even military secrets have been stolen. Laptops present a particular security danger due to their portability. Discuss in small groups what can be done in terms of both physical security and procedures to better protect laptops.

ORGANISATIONAL ISSUES

ACTIVITY 15

What guidelines or rules does your school or college have about computer or Internet use? You probably have Internet usage guidelines, but these are probably more about the things that you should not use the Internet for, than security issues.

In small groups, look at your college or school guidelines and discuss their contents. Why is each guideline required? Do they relate to protecting the security of the system?

Are there any additional guidelines you could propose that relate to the security of the system and individual student accounts?

Produce a student guide to computer security in school/college that could be given to new students at induction.

ACTIVITY 16

Getting people to talk about the computer security tools and measures used in their organisation is difficult since obviously they are sensitive issues and most organisations like to keep the detail confidential. However, you – or your teacher/tutor – may be able to persuade your school or college IT or network manager to talk to you about the measures and tools used in your school or college.

Prepare questions to ask the IT manager about the type and level of threats experienced and the measures taken to protect against them.

ACTIVITY 17

The issue of personal privacy is a growing one. With so much of the detail of our lives recorded on computers, people are concerned that some of it is unnecessary and it could fall into the wrong hands. Carry out some research into the issues, then take part in a group discussion.

Research topics:

British people are under surveillance almost all the time. It is estimated that each person can make up to 300 appearances on CCTV cameras every day. What other ways, apart from CCTV, is information collected about you as you go about your daily life?

The idea of issuing ID cards in the UK has been around for some time, and is a hotly debated topic. What are the current plans for ID cards? What sort of data will be held on the cards? Which other European countries use ID cards?

What laws protect your personal data held on computers? What kind of protection do they provide?

What laws protect content which may be stored on a computer but is created by someone else?

Group discussion topics:

'If you are a law-abiding citizen then you have nothing to fear from the data that is collected about you.' Do you agree with this statement?

Do you think that ID cards are a good idea? What are the benefits and drawbacks of them?

ACTIVITY 18

A friend has had an idea for a piece of software and has begun the development of it. However, your friend does not know how to licence the software when it is complete. Write an explanation for each of the different ways in which software can be licensed, including open source, freeware, shareware and commercial licence. Explain the benefits and drawbacks of each different method of software licensing.

Computer users themselves are often confused about the different types of software licenses. Make a poster that describes the difference between them.

Have you ever read the end-user licence agreement (EULA) of Windows XP? Few people have but you really should know what is says! You can find it in:

C:\windows\system32\eula.txt.

Take a look at the EULA and rewrite its main points in an easy-to-understand format that you could give to a computer user so they know the most important points.

ACTIVITY 19

What does a contract of employment look like? You teacher/tutor should be able to find an example of one. You may also be able to get examples from friends or family, or you might have one of your own from a part-time job. Look at one of the contracts in a small group and discuss what it covers. Is there anything in it about IT security issues? What does the contract say about disciplinary issues related to IT use?

It may well be that the contracts of employment don't say anything specific about IT security issues, although you may find references to confidentiality.

Do you think the contract of employment should be updated to take IT security issues into account?

ACTIVITY 20

In common with many other professions, the computing industry has a number of professional bodies that people with the right qualifications and experience can join (eg The British Computer Society). Find out what professional bodies there are, what the requirements to join them are and what benefits there are joining them. Present your findings in a table.

Some of these professional bodies have codes of conduct or good practice, which govern what is acceptable practice in the industry. Print out at least one of these and discuss in small groups what each point of the code means and how it might be applied in the real world.

There are also two organisations (BSA and FAST) that support the interests of companies that write software, particularly with regard to raising the awareness of copyright abuse (software theft). What do these organisations actually do? How do they encourage awareness of the issue?

MARKED ASSIGNMENTS

UNIT 1 – COMMUNICATION AND EMPLOYABILITY SKILLS FOR IT

Sample assignment	104
Pass level answer	106
Merit level answer	115
Distinction level answer	129

UNIT 3 – INFORMATION SYSTEMS

Sample assignment	135
Pass level answer	137
Pass and Merit level answer	139
Distinction level answer	145
Pass level answer	148

SAMPLE ASSIGNMENT (UNIT 1 (PART))

This assignment addresses the soft skills required by Unit 1. You will undertake a range of tasks that will assist you in meeting the assessment and grading criteria. Each task indicates the criteria addressed. You should undertake every task to the best of your ability if you wish to achieve each criterion involved.

Task 1 (P1)

This is designed to get you to write a personal statement when applying for a post showing how you meet the full person specification set out in the table below. Remember to justify all your statements and assertions. When you have written your personal statement write a brief report (about 150 words – be careful not to use up your word count with unnecessary detail) on why you stressed particular points.

It will allow you to meet criterion P1 'explain why employers value particular employee attributes'. You will need to address all aspects of the content for this criterion. You should also assume, for the purpose of this task, that you have skills in computer hardware and maintenance.

ORGANISATION OVERVIEW

The client specialises in the design, supply and operation of integrated Information and Communication Technology (ICT) solutions. Their innovative solutions harness new technology, enabling significant cost reductions in the supply and management of the ICT infrastructure in an office building. They are now looking to recruit an ICT Technician to provide full internal desktop, network, security and telephony support to occupants of the building. They will provide the right person with additional training.

Key tasks and responsibilities:

You will provide technical and project support on bids and consultancy work as well as on the delivery and maintenance of integrated ICT solutions to clients.

You will also provide remote and on-site IT Helpdesk support to the employees of a charity dedicated to the regeneration of the local community.

The IT support covers all the ICT equipment within the building, including:

- IP CCTV, VOIP, Server 2003, Exchange Server
- Network switches, laptops/desktops, wireless connectivity
- Interactive whiteboards and projectors.

The successful candidate should show evidence of the following **attributes and skills**:

Essential:

- Team player who must have initiative and be able to work unsupervised
- Experience of Wi-Fi
- Working knowledge of Internet/intranet
- Ability to build, repair and maintain computer hardware.

Desirable but not essential:

- Administrative experience of VOIP
- Able to use CAD/AutoCAD
- Knowledge of Microsoft software including Exchange Server, Server 2003, XP and Office 2003/2007.
- Experience of IP networks
- ITIL qualification
- Experience of working in a customer service environment.

104

Task 2 (P6)

In the scenario for the previous task you will see the statement that the organisation offers training for the right person. In order to meet criterion P6, you should produce a table showing your current skills and knowledge matched against the job requirements, the areas of weakness that you feel should be developed in order to meet the person specification, and what sort of training you should undertake in order to gain the necessary skills. Identify whether the training could be carried out internally or externally and describe the skills you might expect of the person delivering the training. Write a brief statement describing all the ways that your training needs might be discovered.

Task 3 (M4 (part))

In order to meet criterion M4 (part), you should prepare and deliver a presentation on learning styles. The presentation may be either a PowerPoint delivery or a series of web pages. Your presentation should identify different approaches to learning and describe the effects of each on the learner. Having completed task 2, you should include slides describing how your own learning style could affect the type of training that you have identified for yourself. Using your knowledge of the Belbin characteristics, add slides showing what you consider to be the learning styles for each of the nine roles and how these could affect team working.

Task 4 (P7, M4 (part), D2)

In order to meet criterion P7, you should prepare and maintain a personal development plan (PDP). You should use your own knowledge and understanding of yourself and your needs as well as information gleaned from your teachers (plus employers and other leaders if possible).

You should start with an initial evaluation of your aims, ambitions and objectives (short, medium and long term) and then set targets. You should update this plan on a regular basis; it will be monitored by your teachers at the end of each academic term.

If you show how the identified goals relate to your learning style, then you could achieve M4 (part). The more detail you put into the plan and the more attention you will pay to it, the more likely you are to achieve criterion D2.

Whether your PDP is created on paper or as soft copy, you must remember to bring it with you to each review session. These review sessions will take place every three months.

The final date for submission of the completed PDP for your two-year programme is 15 June of the second year of study.

Note: You need to complete both task 3 and task 4 in order to stand a chance to achieve M4 fully.

PASS LEVEL ANSWER

Task 1

P1 explain why employers value particular employee attributes
Personal statement Jamila Aitchah

I am a mature person and I have worked previously in a call centre dealing with customer queries on computer systems, this covered both hardware and software problems. Through my employment at this company I have had to work on my own many times but I was promoted to assistant team leader before I left the job to start my full time course. I gained in confidence doing this work as I had to deal with my own calls, problems, logging activities as well as those of the people working for me. I learned to manage my time better when other people relied on me to help them out. Other people say that 'I grew as a person' through doing the job and became more responsible and more reliable. The reference from my previous employer states this. I have also become more even tempered in a stressful environment and am able to deal with all sorts of problems. At home I have built a complete wireless network system for my parents. They have two desktops, and I have a laptop, that use the network. I regularly install new software on the network at home and, of course, I have to maintain the systems so that my parents can carry out their tasks effectively. I am currently completing a BTEC National course in Networking. Part of this course involves setting up and maintaining networks in an office environment. On the course I have gained knowledge in arrangment of MicroSoft operating systems. I understand the current Health and Safety regulations as we have been shown these at College. My previous academic qualifications show that I am literate and numerate.

Explanation

Employers look for people who have the appropriate technical knowledge so I have brought out the aspects in my experience that show this. They should also be made aware of my understanding of working practices and legislation. They look for personal attitudes that will make people easy to work with, who will be able to work with others in the office environment, managing not only their own work but able to help out others.

Employers look for people who are going to work hard and so look for keenness and aptitude. They also look for people who are going to be loyal and stay with the company when fully trained otherwise it can become expensive and time wasting.

Jamila, you have covered a wide range of your skills in this section. Your explanation below shows that you are aware of why you needed to mention your skills and attributes.

What you have written both in the statement and in the explanation is sufficient to gain P1.

Tutor feedback

Task 2
P6 describe ways of identifying and meeting development needs

Aspect	My skills	Training needs
Soft Skills		
Planning	I have some planning skills as I need to schedule the work for my assignments. I used to have to plan rosters and workloads for other people	Once in the job I would need to find out what the job really entailed, what priorities were expected of me and so on. The best way to do this would be by watching a colleague at work and also by asking my line manager. Both these people would need a good understanding of the job and patience to deal with questions.
Organisational Time management	I can follow a plan once I have made it but I may be a bit weak in some areas which would be picked up by line managers through appraisal etc.	These would be addressed on an external training course – someone who does not need to know how the company works.
Team working	The company want someone who is a team player, capable of working on their own I know I can do this but my line manager may indicate that I need to develop certain personal skills	These would be addressed on an external training course – someone who does not need to know how the company works.
Verbal communication Written communication Numeric skills Creativity	I do not believe I have any need for training in any of these. If I did have any weaknesses feedback could come from clients, managers and so on	If courses were necessary then these could be done at a local college.

Jamila

You have related your answer to all aspects of the content. You have done well to personalise the responses and also highlight the relevance to the scenario set.

You have shown your personal skills, trainer skills, internal and external sources of development, and types of training.

Some of your answers are slightly superficial but this answer is sufficient for P6.

107

Aspect	My skills	Training needs
Job specific skills		
Technical knowledge	The company wants a range of skills. Although I have some knowledge of many of these areas I would need training in many. My personal ability would show me my weaknesses as would feedback from colleagues and managers. I also have some personal ambitions to get qualifications from MicroSoft. I want to do these in the next two years.	These would be addressed on external training courses – by someone who does not need to know how the company works. They must of course have an in-depth knowledge of the practical and theory involved in each area. It could require a series of courses to provide more and more detail as time goes by. I do not know what the ITIL qualification is but this would probably be delivered by an external agency such as a local college.
Working procedures involved	I have no knowledge of how the new organisation works, its internal policies etc	The organisation should provide an induction program by a range of staff from different departments; each should be skilled in their own areas but should indicate where their work fits in with other parts of the company. Minor aspects may be met through team meetings.
Health and safety issues	I have an overview of this and other legislation	This area could be merged with the induction programme showing how it fits for the company.

Task 3
M4 explain how individuals can use a knowledge of their learning style to improve their effectiveness in developing new skills or understanding

Learning styles

Jamila Aitchah

Kolb experiential style

- concrete experience,
- observation of and reflection on that experience,
- formation of abstract concepts based upon the reflection,
- testing the new concepts,
- (repeat).

- Learning style theory arose out of the development of magnetic resonance imaging in the early 1980s. As doctors used MRI scanners to treat brain -injured patients, they accumulated a mass of data about how the brain processes information.
- http://education.guardian.co.uk/egweekly/story/0,,1495514,00.htm l

---

My learning style

- I am a kinaesthetic learner – I like to learn by doing
- I would need practical programmes of study
- Just listening to people would be boring and I would not enjoy learning
- I have already found this out on my current course

Visual, Auditory, Kinesthetic (VAK)

- Visual learning (learn by seeing)
- Auditory learning (learn by hearing)
- Kinesthetic learning or practical (learn by doing).

Belbin

- I came out as a team worker as I like being with people and like to share responsibility
- I want to change this otherwise I will never get to be a senior manager

Jamila

This is a very superficial overview of each subject area. It is not at M4 standard yet so I cannot award M4 (part) for this activity. To reach the correct standard you need to read the feedback below very carefully. It is important to answer the questions in the task to make sure that you cover every aspect of the content required.

ASSESSOR FEEDBACK FORM

Jamila

You have given two examples of learning styles but did not discuss how these differ. You have shown your learning style but should have said how you identified it. It is important that you identify the steps taken to reach this decision.

You have not addressed the effects on different learners of their particular learning style. Evidence could have come from a comparison of the different learning styles with job roles. A minimum requirement would have been to show how different people learn. There is insufficient evidence of team working and learning styles. Belbin has a definition of each working preference and each one of these can be related to learning. This could have been emphasised.

Task 4
P7   create and maintain a personal development plan

M4   explain how individuals can use a knowledge of their learning style to improve their effectiveness in developing new skills or understanding

D2   independently use a personal development plan to undergo a process of identification of skill need and related improvement

I have set up a PDP, I started this when I was at school and have kept it going ever since. It is kept on a CD to make it portable from place to place. I did start with a paper version but this became very heavy so I transferred it to CD instead.

I have shown it to my teacher

Three pages from the pdp are included here as samples of the plan developed so far

PDP Jamila Aitchah		
Date of review	1 September	Jamila
Short-term goals	To start BTEC course and succeed in all assignments for first term To manage my time creatively when studying	Very short-term goals but adequate at this stage
Medium-term goals	To finish BTEC course having succeeded in all assignments throughout the course To find a part time job to help support my studies	Medium term covering a two-year period – this might be a slightly long time away but job hunting is in the next six months so that's OK
Long-term goals	To get a successful job that uses all the skills and knowledge that I will have learned through the course. To earn lots of money To be able to help my parents out financially To get married and raise a happy family	Laudable approach to life Let's hope you achieve these
Reflection of progress since last review	I was successful in all my 6 GCSEs that I took but I would like a better mark in Maths so I might see if the College will offer me the chance to see if I can improve my results	Good idea
Review of assignment feedback	My teachers at school were all quite nice and just told me where I was correct but not how to do better	
Action plan	Develop a timetable for studying Sign up for Maths if possible Start looking for part time job	Good start

Tutor feedback

Jamila

I have reviewed your PDP on CD and the sample pages you have provided here. There is sufficient evidence in there to be awarded P7 at the end of the course but read the feedback below for M4 (part) and D2.

111

PDP Jamila Aitchah		
Date of review	1 December	Jamila
Short-term goals	To carry on with BTEC course and succeed in all assignments for second term To improve my time management when studying To start GCSE Maths in January ready for exam in the summer To keep looking for a part time job	Good to see job hunting has moved to short term Added maths here – good follow through
Medium-term goals	To complete GCSE Maths successfully To finish BTEC course having succeeded in all assignments throughout the course	
Long-term goals	To get a successful job that uses all the skills and knowledge that I will have learned through the course To earn lots of money To be able to help my parents out financially To get married and raise a happy family	No change but that's OK at this stage
Reflection of progress since last review	Good, the College will let me do the Maths, start that next month I am having problems fitting the assignments in and getting them done on time with family commitments and religious festivals I have passed all assignments but I know I could do much better – need to work harder to get D level work done Missed out on a couple of Ms as well Long term goals have not changed at all, extra bit in medium and short term	True – there is scope for you to improve the standard of your work
Review of assignment feedback	Some staff are better than others at giving help Feedback for unit 1 is very helpful – I need to be more reflective to reach the higher grades Feedback for unit 2 is not helpful – there are some concepts of hardware that I do not understand – perhaps I need to find a different way of learning for this subject or I need to talk to the teacher to see what I am doing wrong – I cannot learn things in theory, I need to do things Feedback for unit 5 is ok – I understand spreadsheets and I like doing them	You have some good ideas in here and are beginning to show some reflective concepts Make an appointment to see him as soon as possible – do not let things get on top of you!
Action plan	Look out old Maths stuff, revisit to find out where my weaknesses are so I can concentrate on these Have another look at unit 2 work if time before the end of term Have another look at my study plan	Why did you not put need for appointment in here?

PDP Jamila Aitchah		
Date of review	**1 March**	
Short-term goals	To carry on with BTEC course and succeed in all assignments for third term To improve my time management when studying To complete GCSE Maths in the summer	By now I might have expected you to think about adding dates for completion of activities especially assignments as this would help with your planning overall
Medium-term goals	To finish BTEC course having succeeded in all assignments throughout the course	
Long-term goals	To get a successful job that uses all the skills and knowledge that I will have learned through the course To earn lots of money To be able to help my parents out financially To get married and raise a happy family	
Reflection of progress since last review	I have tried to review my study plan but now I have a job at Morrissons I have even less time for my studies Finally finished unit 2 but only got a Pass Unit 5 was a Merit which is good	This is not really reflection but more of a review of progress to date. It is important for the higher criteria that you practise evaluation skills – do not forget to mention this in your later reviews
Review of assignment feedback	I seem to be doing OK in units 6 & 7 and am managing to pick up a couple of Ms and Ds – good support from teacher Hopefully my efforts are beginning to pay off Ought to think about asking for extra time over the holidays to try and get the missing higher grading criteria Not doing so well with unit 18 – cannot understand programming C++, teacher not very helpful, same one as unit 2!	
Action plan	Need to see teacher about unit 18 – book appointment Carry on with unit 1 pdp for next term Do some Maths revision ready for the exam after Easter break	These are only short-term actions It might be appropriate to start thinking about some longer-term ones as well as you are now nearly through the first year of your course What about asking for chance to resubmit some assignments to get higher grades?

ASSESSOR FEEDBACK FORM

Jamila

You have shown short- and medium-term goals for your training and work plans.

Summary records of your academic achievements are in there. You have added to it since you started at college by including any generic feedback from your teachers and discussed assignment grades. You now need to add records of appraisals from your part-time employment.

When you put in evidence from a range of sources it is important that you reflect on this and show how you might change your approach or plans based on feedback from others. You have made an attempt at this.

Bring the CD back to me when you reach the end of your course with us in May next year. Make sure that you highlight skills gained as well as qualifications achieved. (D2)

Include a review of how your learning style has affected the way you have learned and the way you propose to move your career forward based on this. (M4 part)

Keep the short- and medium-term goals updated and, at the end of the course, start to bring in some more long-term goals.

Note to the reader: A good PDP needs to be maintained throughout life. For the purposes of this qualification, one should be started when you start the course. You can use your record of achievement (RoA) from school as a basis but it is important not only to put in what's been done but also to reflect on this to show how patterns and plans might change; you need to become a reflective practitioner.

MERIT LEVEL ANSWER

Task 3

M4 Explain how individuals can use a knowledge of their learning style to improve their effectiveness in developing new skills or understanding.

STUDENT ANSWER

I created and delivered a presentation on learning styles using PowerPoint. I have developed this presentation to detail how awareness of learning style can be used to improve personal effectiveness.

Task 3
Learning styles etc

Contents

- Learning styles
- Visual, Audio, Kinaesthetic
- Honey & Mumford
- Kolb
- Types of training
- How these learning styles can affect individuals' learning and training
- Belbin roles
- My learning style
- My training approaches
- Belbin .v. Learning styles
- Team workers

VAK

When you ...	Visual	Auditory	Kinesthetic
Spell	Do you try to see the word?	Do you sound out the word or use a phonetic approach?	Do you write the word down to find if it feels right?
Talk	Do you talk sparingly but dislike listening for too long? Do you favour words such as *see*, *picture*, and *imagine*?	Do you enjoy listening but are impatient to talk? Do you use words such as *hear*, *tune*, and *think*?	Do you gesture and use expressive movements? Do you use words such as *feel*, *touch*, and *hold*?
Concentrate	Do you become distracted by untidiness or movement?	Do you become distracted by sounds or noises?	Do you become distracted by activity around you?
Meet someone again	Do you forget names but remember faces or remember where you met?	Do you forget faces but remember names or remember what you talked about?	Do you remember best what you did together?
Contact people on business	Do you prefer direct, face-to-face, personal meetings?	Do you prefer the telephone?	Do you talk with them while walking or participating in an activity?
Read	Do you like descriptive scenes or pause to imagine the actions?	Do you enjoy dialogue and conversation or hear the characters talk?	Do you prefer action stories or are not a keen reader?
Do something new at work	Do you like to see demonstrations, diagrams, slides, or posters?	Do you prefer verbal instructions or talking about it with someone else?	Do you prefer to jump right in and try it?
Put something together	Do you look at the directions and the picture?		Do you ignore the directions and figure it out as you go along?
Need help with a computer application	Do you seek out pictures or diagrams?	Do you call the help desk, ask a neighbour, or growl at the computer?	Do you keep trying to do it or try it on another computer?

Tutor feedback

Raphael

You delivered a very good presentation using these slides.

You showed a good insight into the different learning styles and how you relate to them.

You have related these to your own working abilities and your training needs and approaches.

You have also related the generic, theoretical aspects of the learning styles to training that might be appropriate in different situations.

From Honey & Mumford Learning Styles Questionnaire

type	person	Learn best when	Learn less when
activist	Activists like to be involved in new experiences. They are open minded and enthusiastic about new ideas but get bored with implementation. They enjoy doing things and tend to act first and consider the implications afterwards. They like working with others but tend to hog the limelight.	• involved in new experiences, problems and opportunities • working with others in business games, team tasks, role-playing • being thrown in the deep end with a difficult task • chairing meetings, leading discussions	listening to lectures or long explanations reading, writing or thinking on their own absorbing and understanding data following precise instruction to the letter
theorist	Theorists adapt and integrate observations into complex and logically sound theories. They think problems through in a step by step way. They tend to be perfectionists who like to fit things into a rational scheme. They tend to be detached and analytical rather than subjective or emotive in their thinking.	they are put in complex situations where they have to use their skills and knowledge they are in structured situations with clear purpose they are offered interesting ideas or concepts even though they are not immediately relevant they have the chance to question and probe ideas behind things	they have to participate in situations which emphasise emotion and feelings the activity is unstructured or briefing is poor they have to do things without knowing the principles or concepts involved they feel they're out of tune with the other participants e.g. with people of very different learning styles
reflector	Reflectors like to stand back and look at a situation from different perspectives. They like to collect data and think about it carefully before coming to any conclusions. They enjoy observing others and will listen to their views before offering their own.	observing individuals or groups at work they have the opportunity to review what has happened and think about what they have learned producing analyses and reports doing tasks without tight deadlines	acting as leader or roleplaying in front of others doing things with no time to prepare being thrown in at the deep end being rushed or worried by deadlines
pragmatist	Pragmatists are keen to try things out. They want concepts that can be applied to their job. They tend to be impatient with lengthy discussions and are practical and down to earth.	there is an obvious link between the topic and job they have the chance to try out techniques with feedback e.g. role-playing they are shown techniques with obvious advantages e.g. saving time they are shown a model they can copy e.g. a film or a respected boss	there is no obvious or immediate benefit that they can recognise there is no practice or guidelines on how to do it there is no apparent pay back to the learning e.g. shorter meetings in the event or learning is 'all theory'

Cartoons reproduced by permission of the Campaign for Learning.

VAK summary

- Visual
  - Likes to learn by looking and watching
  - Would be happy to watch training videos and shadowing activities

- Auditory
  - Likes to learn by listening and talking
  - Would be happy attending training courses with theory and discussion sessions, might be ok with staff meetings

- Kinaesthetic
  - Likes to learn by trying things out
  - Would be happiest when given practical tasks to do in training sessions but might prefer to try first before attending training

Honey & Mumford summary

- Activist
  - Likes to learn the hard way by doing things straight away
  - Would be happiest when given practical tasks to do in training sessions but might prefer to try first before attending training
- Theorist
  - Likes to learn by thinking through a problem and working it out for themselves, alone
  - Probably would not appreciate any training
- Reflector
  - Likes to work slowly through problems from different aspects especially watching others
  - Could be trained through job shadowing and staff meetings
- Pragmatist
  - Likes to build on prior skills and experience to save time and energy
  - Probably would not appreciate any training but would settle on what ever was provided just to get on with the job

Kolb summary

- Diverger
  - Likes to work slowly through problems from different aspects
  - Probably would not appreciate any training

- Assimilator
  - Likes to work through problems from different aspects, can develop new ideas
  - Could be trained through job shadowing and staff meetings and would then see better ways of doing things

- Converger
  - Likes to learn by thinking through a problem, can develop new ideas
  - Probably would not appreciate any training but would sit quietly and come up with alternative approaches to the job

- Accommodator
  - Likes to build on prior skills and experience
  - Probably would not appreciate any training but would settle on what ever was provided just to get on with the job

Possible types of training available

- In house sessions
- Staff meetings
- Electronic packages
- External formal courses
- Job shadowing

You managed to answer the questions about how knowledge of learning styles shows how people can improve their effectiveness in self development by finding training programmes that best suit their own approach to learning, eg use of e-learning for those who prefer to learn alone (especially when gaining experience of new software), ie visual learner, pragmatist, accommodator.

You answered all of the questions posed showing that you understood the underlying material and concepts.

You have also related Belbin's team worker profile to different training approaches as well as your own.

Your presentation was clear and thoughtful.

Belbin

Plant
PL
The Innovator. Unorthodox, knowledgeable and imaginative, turning out loads of radical ideas. The creative engine-room that needs careful handling to be effective. Individualistic, disregarding practical details or protocol – can become an unguided missile.

Resource Investigator
RI
The extrovert, enthusiastic communicator, with good connections outside the team. Enjoys exploring new ideas, responds well to challenges, and creates this attitude amongst others. Noisy and energetic, quickly loses interest, and can be lazy unless under pressure.

Chairman
CH
Calm, self-confident and decisive when necessary. The social leader of the group, ensuring individuals contribute fully, and guiding the team to success. Unlikely to bring great intellect or creativity.

Shaper
SH
Energetic, highly-strung, with a drive to get things done. They challenge inertia, ineffectiveness and complacency in the team, but can be abrasive, impatient and easily provoked. Good leaders of start-up or rapid-response teams.

EXTROVERT ROLES – outward looking people whose main orientation is to the world outside the group, and beyond the task(s) in hand.

Belbin

Monitor Evaluator
ME

Unemotional, hardheaded and prudent. Good at assessing proposals, monitoring progress and preventing mistakes. Dispassionate, clever and discrete. Unlikely to motivate others, takes time to consider, may appear cold and uncommitted. Rarely wrong.

Team Worker
TW

Socially-oriented and sensitive to others. Provides an informal network of communication and support that spreads beyond the formal activities of the team. Often the unofficial or deputy leader, preventing feuding and fragmentation. Concern for team spirit may divert from getting the job done.

Company Worker
CW

The organiser who turns plans into tasks. Conservative, hard-working, full of common sense, conscientious and methodical. Orthodox thinks who keeps the team focussed on the tasks in hand. Lacks flexibility, and unresponsive to new ideas

Completer Finisher
CF

Makes sure the team delivers. An orderly, anxious perfectionist who worries about everything. Maintains a permanent sense of urgency that can sometimes help and sometimes hinder the team. Good at follow-up and meeting deadlines

INTROVERT ROLES – inward-looking people principally concerned with relations and tasks within the group.

My learning styles

- Based on the VAK approach
  - Mostly visual with a hint of kinaesthetic

- Based on Honey & Mumford
  - Mostly a theorist

- Based on Kolb
  - Essentially an assimilator

- Summary
  - I like to think carefully and read around a subject before making a decision

My training approaches

- I am quite happy to look things up for myself and read subjects

- I could use elearning for training or read manuals

- In the previous task I identified a need to gain training for ITIL
  - there are some elearning courses for this that I would ask to use

- Any knowledge in new software and hardware can be got through reading manuals

Belbin .v. learning styles

- When I did the Belbin test I came out as an introvert, mostly monitor/evaluator
- The Kolb learning style for this is probably a converger
- The Honey and Mumford style for this is likely to be a theorist
- The VAK style is mostly visual
- Summary
  - I fit with H&M & VAK but not with Kolb
  - This will still match with my approach to study
  - I could have problems in some jobs but for the IT technician role my approach is likely to be suitable as users will need to be happy that their problems are corrected
  - I can work unsupervised but am not a real team player but I do have initiative

Team workers

- A team worker should have the following skills:
  - Be able to mix with others
  - Be able to support outside of the team
  - Act as an arbitrator
- But may not always help get the job done properly
- The Kolb learning style for this is probably a cross between an accommodator and a diverger
- The Honey and Mumford style for this is likely to be a activist
- The VAK style is likely to be mostly kinaesthetic with a bit of visual
- Summary
  - This shows that I am not likely to be a true team worker because I do not match with any of the learning styles involved

PDP

- KISS SMART

- Keep It Simple Sunshine by setting Specific, Measurable, Achievable, Realistic and Timely goals

- Running this as a blog updated each week

Tutor feedback

Note, that this feedback should also act as a witness statement to address those aspects of learning styles not directly evidenced by the slides' content

F Ogunye (Miss)

fpo@mycollege.ac.uk

DISTINCTION LEVEL ANSWER

Task 4
D2   Use a personal development plan independently to identify skill needed and related improvement.

I have maintained a blog, monitoring my work on my Personal Development Plan.

My learning blog.

The following is an extract from my blog PDP showing my application of Keep It Simple Sunshine by setting Specific, Measurable, Achievable, Realistic and Timely goals principles (KISS SMART)

Week 1

I am just about to choose my GCSE programme of study. I think I would do best with Maths, English, Science, IT, Business Studies but I will have to see what others fit into the timetable. I want to be able to do 8 subjects in total. My SAT scores have been good so far, I am proud of my achievements.

.

.

Week 12

Not sure that I like Geog & History but will carry on as these are the only ones that did not involve too much practical work or physical activity! Citizenship Studies is really common sense so I should be OK there. My teachers say that I am doing well in the main subjects I chose.

.

.

Week 105

The 6th form teachers have allowed me to take the BTEC ITP programme provided that I get at least a C grade in Maths, English and IT plus one other subject. My year tutor says that my current progress means I should get these grades. The exams were not too bad so I will have to sit back and wait until August to see what the grades really are. Need to get a job over the holidays to earn some cash.

Week 112

Took a few weeks off from the blog but just want to record now that I got the grades I needed. In fact I got A* in Maths and IT and all the other grades were Bs and Cs so I did OK – now to celebrate!! Good that Morrison's gave me a job for the holidays.

Week 114

Have just started the course. Teachers seem OK, currently studying units 1, 2 and 3. They have given us a reading list. I shall work out a schedule for studying the material. Morrison's are allowing me to work part time at the weekends so the schedule must be built in around that. Need to learn my way round all the rooms and get to know new staff. Get a map and an internal directory off the intranet!

Week 115

Have been handed three assignments this week. The one for unit 2 is easy – just need to find some suitable web sites to look at – this has to be done in two weeks time. The one for unit 3 is about business functions – easy! – have already done this last year at school so shall re-read that material and update. The one for unit 1 is to set up a PDP. Shall ask Miss Ogunye if my blog is good enough. Have to decide on my goals in life!? What do I want to do?

- Succeed on the course, (medium term)
- pass all assignments with good grades, (short to medium term)
- go to university and (long term)
- Get a good job
- Be happy

Have to hand this in next week. Am going to maintain this blog from now on using

- KISS SMART principles
- Keep It Simple Sunshine by setting Specific, Measurable, Achievable, Realistic and Timely goals

To do – make appointment with Miss O; write up goals; start work on units 2 & 3 assignments.

Week 116

Spoke to Miss O, she said my blog was a bit informal but providing that I covered all the required content it could be OK. I have added a to-do list each week to set myself very short term goals and help me manage my time properly. I now have to look at different learning styles and judge what mine are. I have decided that I do not like group work very much, hate relying on others who do not seem to work as hard as I do! I am NOT a team worker but this is a skill I must definitely practise if I want to pass this course. I need to find time to sit and read about different styles, the web will be the place to start. Must finish unit 2 assignment by Monday – nearly done, must remember to put in bibliography!

To do – finish and hand in unit 2 assignment; continue working on unit 3 one; investigate learning styles etc

Week 117

Handed in unit 2 assignment – feedback says I passed all criteria – teacher says I am working at D level so far – this is good. So one of my goals is getting there – just got to keep it up now. Need to finish unit 3 assignment for Monday. Just got to finalise the diagrams for data flow. Learning styles are quite interesting – have seen that my dislike of group work means I am not really a team player in Belbin rules but I am a visual learner (according to VAK principles)as I like to read and find out for myself a lot – could have told them that anyway but at least I know who I am! Got an interview with my personal tutor on Wednesday. What's that all about?

To do – finish and hand in unit 3 assignment; write up findings on learning styles; plan for interview

Week 118

Still waiting for feedback on unit 3 assignment, think it was ok though. Interview was interesting, he wanted to make sure I was coping on the course and to review my blog – see signature above – next meeting in 4 weeks time so I must keep updating the blog! Tutor said that I needed to try to work as a member of a team more (true but hard with some of my classmates!). He is pleased with my progress so far. My parents have planned a holiday for half term so need to keep ahead of my work! Need to check with teachers to see if any other assignments are due soon and what I can be reading about while away. Got next assignment for unit 2 this week – seems to build on work from the other one so should be OK – need to get some specifications for different computers – plenty on the web.

Need to hand in first assignment for unit 1 on Tuesday – must finish writing up. Not really sure what this has to do with IT but shall wait for the light to dawn! Morrison's want me to go on to work on the tills but I have no experience of this except a couple of hours shadowing Freda. There is a till training course in three weeks time, which may mean missing some classes. I need to check my schedule and let the teachers know. Although shadowing is fine for my learning style I think I might need a more practical approach this time to get the extra skills (not something that could be done by reading or watching a video!)

New medium term goal – to become a till supervisor!

To do – finish and hand in unit 1 assignment; find suitable web sites; make appointments to see all teachers; try harder at group work; check timetable; confirm ok with teachers to go on course

Monthly summary – 1

Short term – am passing my assignments with good marks; so far therefore will keep this as a short term goal for the next month

Medium term – if the assignments are being passed then progress is being made with the success on the course

New medium term goal – to become a till supervisor (but not until I have lots of experience of the job!)

Long term – remains the same

New short term goal – try and change hatred of group work; pass till training course

[several weeks omitted from blog]

Monthly summary – 6

Short term – assignments – I am passing my assignments with good marks; so far therefore will keep this as a short term goal for the next month

Short term – group work – doing much better now and am beginning to contribute more and control the way that my classmates work

Medium term – if the assignments are being passed then progress is being made with the success on the course

Medium term goal – to become a till supervisor – getting there, gaining the experience and my line manager says I am doing very well so far

Long term – remains the same

Week 141

Have just been given two programming assignments, one for Java and one for C++. My current experience is only SQL & macros (VBA) through Access. I am finding these two units quite hard as they are introducing concepts that I have not experienced so far! Have bought some textbooks and student editions of the software for my home computer so I can practice, there is not enough time on the college computers. The two languages are both similar and different in the coding so it is hard to tell one structure from another sometimes everything else going quite well actually, have passed all last semester's units with D grades (except unit 1 because we do not get the final grade till the end of the course.

New short term goal – learn the two languages and how to distinguish between them.

Raphael

This is the 4th time that you and I have met.

You are maintaining this blog each week very studiously by yourself. Miss Ogunye and I only monitor the activity but do not contribute to it.

Each time we meet you are showing that you are fully aware of your strengths and weaknesses – reports from your other teachers show that you have made great headway in learning how to work as a member of a group and are now beginning to become a leader rather than just an individual.

You have learned many new software skills for which you should be very proud.

You have clearly identified several skills and experience weaknesses esp. programming. You have shown how you propose to get round these weaknesses.

Your current grades for the first semester show that, providing you maintain the same standard, you should gain an overall Distinction for the course BUT you must not let these standards slip at all!

jmx@mycollege.ac.uk

[several weeks omitted from blog]

Week 168

New year started here. Passed last year's units with D grades; now have to choose university programmes – that means deciding on what I would like to do as a job. Things have been going well at Morrison's – I am now a till supervisor (got promoted over the summer!) – and quite like the management even though it does not really suit what I thought my learning style was last year. I must have changed! Think I will opt for something like Business information Management – need to seek out possible options of courses.

New short term goal – fill in UCAS forms

To do – talk to careers teacher about degree options

Monthly summary – 13

Short term – assignments – am passing my assignments with good marks; so far therefore will keep this as a short term goal for the next month

Medium term – if the assignments are being passed then progress is being made with the success on the course – now becomes short term

Medium term goal – to become a till supervisor – getting there, gaining the experience and my line manager says I am doing very well so far – success – done it

Short term goal – fill in UCAS forms

Long term – get to university becomes medium term

Long term – succeed at university and get a good job

[several weeks omitted from blog]

Raphael

You have worked consistently very hard throughout the course. All your teachers have given you excellent reports showing that you have improved your academic skills and developed as a person. You have shown a very good understanding of your learning methods and how these affect your work. Your supervisor at your place of work also gave you an excellent record, congratulations for making senior till supervisor, by the way! He said that you learned a lot whilst you were there over the past two years and that they are glad to sponsor your course at university. You have maintained this log independently showing how goals can change, be added to as new problems come along and be deleted when achieved.

jmx@mycollege.ac.uk

Week 176

Passed the course, got overall Distinction in every unit – just need to wait and see what this one remaining assignment gives me. Have got place at Manchester University to study Business Management, have got sponsorship from Morrison's as my line manager gave me a glowing reference

New goal – succeed on uni course, keep up log

Raphael

Although I was dubious to begin with when you asked if you could adopt this approach (more of a diary than a plan) it clearly demonstrates a plan-do-review technique. The informality embeds mapping of goals, setting of timescales for achievement and reflection. The to-do list each week with follow-up is laudable. P7 is awarded to you because you started this and kept it up all the time.

You have shown where your learning style fits into your studies and work life and the presentation for task 3 enhances this. Therefore I will award the part of M4 available in this assignment, the knowledge you showed in the presentation covers the rest of M4 and so you have achieved M4 overall.

The independence that you have shown in maintaining this blog throughout your time at college, the fact that you have identified academic and work based skills needs, obtained good feedback from all your teachers showing that you have worked towards all your goals and development needs together means that you have achieved D2.

SAMPLE ASSIGNMENT (UNIT 3 (PART))

This assignment addresses the knowledge of information sources, collection, issues and constraints required by Unit 3. You will undertake a range of tasks that will assist you in meeting the assessment and grading criteria. Each task indicates the criteria addressed. You should undertake every task to the best of your ability if you wish to achieve each criterion involved.

You should read the following scenario carefully and ensure that you relate all your answers it.

Scenario

Ubiquitous Bargains

Ubiquitous Bargains (UB) is a retail organisation that sells a range of goods, mostly clothing. Within the organisation are a range of departments whose line managers report to the managing director.

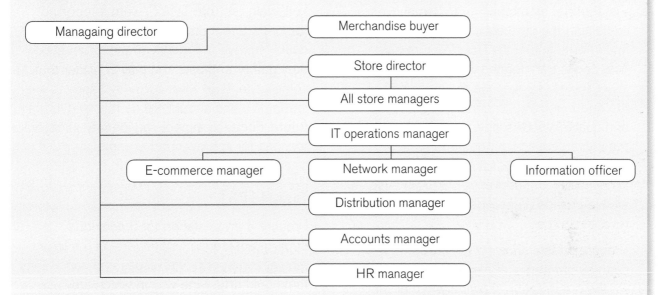

The information officer's role is to ensure that business information and company information is readily available to everyone in UB who needs it and that the information supplied is accurate, timely, relevant and consistent. The information officer (Jamal) also searches for data on UB's competitors' results and progress.

In-store buyers can see what garments (including size and colour) were sold when and where, and whether they had to be discounted to achieve the sale. What sold last year is not necessarily an accurate guide to what will sell in the coming season but it is, nevertheless, a useful input into the buying decision.

For a retail organisation the basic requirement is the appropriate analysis of sales – who is buying, what they are buying, when they are buying, the cost of sales, the stock lead-times and so on. The policy on business information is to have a single source and that is the data warehouse. All sales data from the EPOS system is loaded onto the data warehouse.

Centralising sales and related data on the data warehouse goes at least halfway to ensuring accuracy and consistency. The other half of the story is to ensure that the enquiry/report generator software is used correctly, and the Information Group includes staff who are available to advise, help and audit the use of company information.

UB has opted for an extensive website that catalogues most of its products, each with a picture and description. This has increased their sales by 200%.

Another area of information is company information: boardroom developments, company statistics, personnel information, policy and procedures and so on. As with most companies, UB had large amounts of paper and manuals. Often they were not available to those who needed the information and, where information was available, it was very possibly not the latest version. All this company information is now on an intranet supplemented by email notifications of significant changes. The use of an intranet does not ensure that the information is up-to-date but it does make sure that everyone can access the latest version.

Task 1 (P1)

a Write a brief memorandum to Jamal explaining the difference between data and information in the UB structure and how one is transformed into the other. You should also describe the meanings of the terms primary, secondary, quantitative and qualitative. Describe, in general, the characteristics of good information, considering timeline, accuracy, sufficiency, accessibility and relevance (TASAR). Also, please provide a description of what is a reliable source.

b Prepare a table showing the different sources of internal and external information for the organisation showing whether the information is qualitative or quantitative, whether it is a primary or secondary source, and its characteristics. For the characteristics you should consider timeline, accuracy, sufficiency, accessibility and relevance (TASAR). Please identify and describe three internal and two external sources.

Task 2 (M1)

Add to the table, created in Task 1b, an extra column, or write a report to identify why it is important to have an effective collection process for the information being sought. You should also show how different departments, within the organisation, could make more appropriate use of the information.

Task 3 (D1)

Following on from Task 2, write a report to the department managers showing how each could improve the quality of the information they gather and use. You may consider that some aspects of what currently happens are ineffective and should not be followed in the future. For each aspect you identify, justify your reasons for improvement or removal.

Task 4 (P5)

Prepare a presentation for the various department/section managers on the legal, ethical and operational issues and constraints that could affect the way in which they use customer information, and describe how these may impact on the organisation.

You could include aspects such as:

• The data protection act
• The privacy and electronic communications regulations
• The computer misuse act
• Costing and planning
• Training
• Security and back-up

You should deliver the presentation to your tutor to ensure that it is fit for purpose to be shown to the UB staff.

PASS LEVEL ANSWER

Task 1a

Memo

To: Jamal

From: Ricky

Subject: Data .v. information

Raw data are numbers, characters, images or other outputs from devices to convert physical quantities into symbols, in a very broad sense. Such data are typically further processed by a human or input into a computer, stored and processed there, or transmitted (output) to another human or computer. *Raw data* is a relative term; data processing commonly occurs by stages, and the "processed data" from one stage may be considered the "raw data" of the next. (Wikipedia definition)

For UB this could include the collection of data from the different stores on the numbers of certain items of clothing sold each week. This needs to be done with an effective collection process and stored in a meaningful way so that it can be processed when required. This would be primary data whereas secondary data could come from external sources such as other companies' financial reports, stock exchange data or government information. It is likely that the raw data collected internally would be quantitative as it would be facts and figures. The data collected from external sources is more likely to be qualitative as it could come in the form of textual reports and would need transforming into material that could be used in house. The external facts and figures such as census data, that UB might care to use perhaps when deciding where to open up a new store, would be quantitative.

Information is data that are processed into something meaningful to the reader or audience. This can involve using additional data from other sources such as costings and possible delivery times from suppliers.

The different methods of transforming the data into information could include the production of charts and graphs so that the results are easily visible to the reader. (Accessibility) Each of the sets of results must be clearly related to the needs of the

This is a very succinct definition (remember to cite and reference more fully in future).

You have related the theory to the scenario and shown how the data can become information.

A diagram might have been helpful.

You have addressed the general content for this aspect of the criterion.

This is sufficient for P1a.

You might care to present this as evidence towards unit 1 – check with the tutor for that unit – but it might need putting into a house style first.

PASS LEVEL ANSWER

particular department requesting the information so that they are not confused by information that is irrelevant to their needs. (Relevance)

The result of processing the store data together with the supplier data, as identified above, will give management and buyers details on what is selling well, how much it costs to make and how far in advance distribution orders must be placed to make sure that the stores never run out of supplies.

The source data should always be made up from current figures, in this instance, otherwise the information produced would be of no use to management and buyers. (Timeline) The source data must also always be correct and adequate in quantity otherwise the information produced could be wrong or insufficiently detailed and therefore give a faulty impression to the reader. (Accuracy, Sufficiency)

Reliable sources are ones that the reader can trust at all times. Hopefully all internally generated data will be reliable as it will be UB systems and staff that generate them. Many web based sources may have no provenance as the web is open to anyone to add pages, e.g. Wikipedia. Government-based and competitor sources may be biased and may feed the reader misinformation.

I hope that this is a sufficient explanation, please feel free to come back to me if not.

PASS AND MERIT LEVEL ANSWER

Task 1b and 2

	Internal data sources
Source	1 Orders placed on the web (sales department)
Primary or secondary	Primary
Qualitative or quantitative	Quantitative
Timeliness	Always up to date and added to previous orders placed
Accuracy	Depends on skills of buyer when using the web page
Sufficiency	Providing the web form asks for appropriate details the data will be sufficient
Accessibility	Required by warehouse staff to make sure they can fill order
Relevance	Extremely important as it shows online orders placed (numbers and items)
Usefulness as information when processed	To UB this is vital data – they can use it to show web sales against store sales (sales have gone up 200%). It is very important that the web based form is properly designed to get all the detail needed by the distribution department to be able to ship the correct order in a timely manner to the customer.
Effectiveness	Use of a web page is a very effective manner to collect data from a cost point of view, the only costs are setting up the form and the programmes that will process into information (both one off costs), the only time is that of the customer placing the order. The data gathered are available through the computers to every department that might wish to use them. The day to day use of the processed information involves three departments – sales, purchases and distribution. Over time the sales department (stores) will be able to see items that do not sell quickly and be able to apply in store discounts if necessary. The distribution department will be able to tell which a Items are blocking the warehouse and make suggestions for online discounts. The accounts department will process the figures on a monthly or quarterly basis to be able to see profit and loss information.

Ricky

Source I1

Good

TASAR principles discussed with reasons (sometimes brief but sufficient).

Valid point here.

Good concepts – picked up points from scenario here.

You have now related the theory to the case study.

This section is a good answer and working well towards Merit level work.

You have shown relevance to several departments and indicated what they could do with the information extracted.

	Internal (I) data sources
Source	2 staff hours worked from HR department
Primary or secondary	Primary
Qualitative or quantitative	Quantitative
Timeliness	Collected on a daily or weekly basis to use when calculating payroll so always up to date
Accuracy	This depends on the method of collection Swipe cards will give computerized collection methods which should be tamperproof but hand written may be lies or forged data
Sufficiency	Providing done each day by all staff then each week's figures will be sufficient
Accessibility	If computerized, the data will always be available but if hand written then it could get lost
Relevance	To individual staff the data are very important otherwise they won't get paid. To UB it's also very important as they need to know their outgoing costs
Usefulness as information when processed	The data collected are very useful and could be used for a range of purposes but will show immediately how many staff are working and how many hours each does. Longer term information purposes include scope for pay rises, need to reduce staff numbers, redeployment and so on.
Effectiveness	The effectiveness of the data collection technique depends very much on whether it is by hand or computerised. UB would be better off using a computerised approach to the collection for two reasons, data can easily be made available to other departments in the organisation and fewer errors will be made in the collection of it. In this way it can be processed more quickly into meaningful information for several different departments

Source I2

TASAR principles applied OK.

You have now related the theory to the case study.

Some valid points raised throughout.

These two sections are jumbled up a bit but overall the points are at Merit level.

You have suggested ways in which the organisation can use the information and how to improve the collection method.

	Internal data sources
Source	3 accounts statistical reports
Primary or secondary	Secondary
Qualitative or quantitative	Both – quantitative from figures produced but qualitative from interpretation, charts etc
Timeliness	Probably produced once or twice a year, always after the time during which the data was originally collected
Accuracy	This depends very much on what statistical approaches are taken to produce the reports
Sufficiency	The data used to prepare the reports is sufficient to get the information shown
Accessibility	The reports are available to a range of readers especially all relevant stakeholders
Relevance	The reports have been produced with relevant stakeholders in mind and meet their needs. The reports are also used to present a favourable view of UB to competitors
Usefulness as information when processed	Usefulness as information when processed Can be used to compare year on year progress, profits etc Can boost market sales if buyers see UB in a favourable light
Effectiveness	Providing each department submits its figures in a timely manner the reports produced will be valid but if they do not then there will be discrepancies when comparisons year on year are made

Source I3

The points here are of the same standard as source I2.

You have now related the theory to the case study.

This is a valid point.

Quite right but why cannot the accounts department collect the data rather than waiting for submission?

141

	External (E) data sources
Source	1 telephone questionnaire commissioned to external marketing organisation by the organisation comparing UB with other organisations
Primary or secondary	Primary
Qualitative or quantitative	Both Quantitative when answers done on numeric basis and qualitative when opinions asked (free speech)
Timeliness	To undertake such a poll requires much planning so results cannot be expected immediately
Accuracy	Depends on truth given by respondents
Sufficiency	Only if big enough poll done to give reliable results

Source E1

This is an interesting concept.

You have now related the theory to the case study.

	External (E) data sources – CONTINUED
Accessibility	Easy for respondent as only requires time to give answers, questioner needs computer to store results that can then be easily processed into information
Relevance	Based on questions asked the processed information will be relevant to UB
Usefulness as information when processed	This will depend on who designs the questionnaire. Often this is done by the marketing company rather than the host organisation so UB may lose some control over the results then come from the poll. Dependent on questions asked the results can be used in sales, purchasing, distribution and marketing departments to see how the customers perceive the organisation.
Effectiveness	As a data collection method this will depend on the people contacted. In order to get a range of results the company used to do the poll must be told to get feedback from a cross section of the public. To get decent results that UB can use UB people must be involved in the development f the questionnaire.

Definitely.

This work is all at Merit standard.

	External data sources
Source	2 other organisations' sales data
Primary or secondary	Secondary
Qualitative or quantitative	Both – quantitative figures and qualitative reports
Timeliness	Usually produced on an annual basis and available to external readers through published annual reports
Accuracy	Figures can be checked but may have hint of bias
Sufficiency	Will be superficial in that detailed results of individual items may not be present
Accessibility	Not in format easy to incorporate into UB reports as probably pdf or such on the web or hard copy
Relevance	Gives good opportunity to compare overall favourability and achievement between similar organisations.
Usefulness as information when processed	Outcomes can be incorporated into UB company reports. Information helps UB decide how they are doing in the marketplace compared with others. Useful to sales, accounts
Effectiveness	Easy to collect providing UB knows the names of all its competitors but as with UB's own reports the statistics reported must be regarded as being very biased.

Source E2

You have now related the theory to the case study.

You have made some valid points here and in conjunction with other 4 sources show an understanding of the collection and use of data when processed into information.

Therefore, in summary, it can be seen from the above tables how important the effective data collection, processing and usage of the derived information can be.

UB currently has a centralised storage for the data collected internal to the organisation; it also has a report generator to extract the information required by the different departments. Jamal is responsible for seeking out information from external sources that might be useful to UB personnel.

If the data collection process does not operate properly then the data collected could be false and useless to UB, it could lead to wrong results being generated and therefore cause loss of business or money.

If Jamal is not selective in the information he gathers from external sources then he could feed into the system inaccurate results which, in turn, could lead to errors. He could also generate information through analysis of external sources which could be useful to competitors thus losing competitive advantage in the field for UB.

The information is extracted (processed) through the report generator. UB appears to let individuals use this even though they might not be experienced. It is important that all users of the system understand how it works and what information can be gathered from the data stored. If the processing of the data is not done correctly then the information produced could be inappropriate and meaningless to the chosen audience.

The different department managers will use the information for purposes such as monitoring what happens in their departments (e.g. the HR department can see where the wage bills are going; the sales department will be able to spot trends showing the best selling items; store managers will be able to make day to day decisions about the way their store is running; the board will be able to make medium and long term decisions about the company operation e.g. building new stores or closing existing ones). Whatever individuals do with the information it should always be for the best interests of UB in helping them gain competitive advantage over their rivals. If the data collected are not appropriate, accurate, sufficient, up-to-date and relevant, if the processing is not carried out properly then the information will not be useful – therefore all individuals in UB must operate effectively to aid the company.

ASSESSOR FEEDBACK FORM

Ricky

You have done well to match the theoretical aspects to the scenario throughout your discussion in the above tables. Overall your tables show that you have addressed internal and external data sources and the characteristics of the data collected. Therefore you have met P1.

The additional rows in your tables plus the long summary that follows give enough detail to allow M1 to be awarded as well. You have shown clearly how business can be compromised if collection, processing and usage are not effective within UB. You have also demonstrated, with examples, where the information can be used effectively.

DISTINCTION LEVEL ANSWER

Task 3
Report to department managers

This report should be read in conjunction with the summary above and the memo to Jamal.

UB runs a centralised database on which all internal data are stored. Therefore it should always be possible to produce reliable information from the data stored. This will not always be possible when obtaining external data and information.

Each department must be totally responsible for the data it collects and processes. Internally it is vital that each department identifies the type of information required for their own and other departments' needs. Then the programmes, using the report generator, can make sure that the results are valid and reliable.

It is also important to make sure that only correct personnel get to see information that is relevant to them. This will prevent errors creeping into the data stored. The data stored must be fully protected against internal and external threats. This can be done by using security checks and software protection such as firewalls. In this way the data will remain reliable and produce valid information.

When collecting data from customers it is important to make sure that UB follows the Data Protection regulations but reliable facts can only be collected if the correct questions are asked of people. So UB must make sure that planning tales place before questions are asked. Online ordering forms must be made as simple as possible to use so that customers do not get bored filling in the forms and drop out before orders are complete. The ordering system must not update any figures until the order is confirmed and paid for otherwise the stock details may be inaccurate. The HR department must provide online collection of hours worked so that staff can be paid on time and the correct monies involved are calculated.

Gathering data and information from external sources must be done thoughtfully as published information will always have a bias and also might not come from reliable sources. The use of statistics can be manipulated to give results the producer wants to see rather than the truth.

All aspects of management must make sure they understand the use of business information, how to read the reports produced and make decisions based on these and what detail should be ignored or treated with caution.

Ricky

You have made valid points about protecting the data as this will help ensure the correct business information can be produced.

You have followed through from the previous task very well, picking up the current data collection undertaken.

You have discussed where possible adjustments to current procedures could take place.

145

Recommendations

1. Collection
   a. Ensure that Jamal is fully aware of the types of external information required to assist in the operation of UB
   b. Ensure that on line ordering system is designed with the customer in mind
   c. Ensure that all departments (including the stores) undertake any data collection activities on a regular basis (this may be daily, weekly etc depending on the need for the information extracted)
2. Processing
   a. Ensure that all personnel accessing information from the centralised system through the report generator have training in the use of the system
   b. Ensure that all personnel accessing information know what information they need to get for their purposes
   c. Ensure that information is only available to those who need it
3. Usage
   a. Ensure that all decisions are made based only on the information extracted (both current and historical from the data warehouse)
   b. Ensure that all information is only for the benefit of UB and not disclosed to competitors

Reasons

1. Collection
   To ensure that the data collected meets the TASAR principles
2. Processing
   To ensure that the business information extracted can be used in an appropriate manner by the correct personnel
3. Usage
   To ensure senior management have sufficient information to make strategic decisions
   To ensure a more effective use of the business information towards gaining a greater competitive advantage over rivals

Approaches

- Provide training to all personnel concerned based on the eight points listed above

- Have regular meetings between department managers and the information officer to ensure collection techniques are appropriate, timely and valid; to ensure that all concerned know how to collect, process and use information

- Involve senior management in the regular meetings to ensure the business information they receive from department managers is fit for their purposes

ASSESSOR FEEDBACK FORM

Ricky

You have addressed the areas pertinent to UB. You have given reasons for your recommendations to aid improvement in data collection, processing and usage. Each of these will support the business information produced by UB to be more appropriate and relevant in achieving competitive advantage. The approaches were not requested but show an insight into business functionality. This work is at Distinction level; therefore you have achieved D1.

PASS LEVEL ANSWER

Task 4

UB organisational policy recommendations

Computer misuse act

- It is illegal to hack into anyone else's data
- This means that the IT department must ensure that the data stored is kept very secure so hackers cannot access it
- It must also prevent staff being able to 'hack out' when searching for information on competitors' results – only published data must be used when preparing reports
- It is also illegal to use copies of software that have not been directly purchased with sufficient licences
- This means that the IT department must prevent other personnel load any software that has not been purchased by the company

Data Protection Act

- The act has 8 principles regarding the collection and use of data and information for people.
- This will affect store managers if they collect credit/debit card details from people
- It was also affect HR department when they store details of employees
- Great care must be taken to ensure that the details remain safe and not visible to anyone outside of UB
- The details must not be sold on without the prior permission of the people concerned

Health and safety

- This act requires that UB will make all their offices and stores safe places to work in
- All staff must be made aware of their individual responsibilities in the work place
- This must be done through training
- H&S officers must be appointed on every site including stores and offices to look after general problems
- Logs must be set up to report and track problems raised by staff
- IT staff need to ensure that any equipment is installed appropriately in line with the legislation

Ricky,

You have addressed sufficient constraints as required by the assignment.

The slides are well organised and the presentation structure is fine. An introductory slide to indicate what is going to be contained in the rest of the slides is always useful.

The delivery of the presentation did show that you had a better understanding of the legal issues that are detailed here.

It was clear that you had included health and safety for completeness, even though its direct relevance to the use of customer information is limited.

Privacy and electronic communications

- These regulations deal essentially with how UB would conduct their e-marketing
- Full details of the organisation must be supplied when approaching potential or existing clients either by phone or email
- This means that all ecommerce activities must follow the guidelines
- An extension of this could involve the internal electronic communications such as email
- Email etiquette is becoming a vital aspect to consider – no insults, no slander or libel
- This means that all company personnel must receive training in effective email techniques

Costing and planning

- IT costs are going down but equipment needs are going up
- In order to keep abreast of changes in hw and sw it is vital to make sure all is up to date
- UB should create a rolling plan of upgrades across the organisation
- Any time a new shop is set up new equipment will be needed
- When doing this it is important to check that the licences are still sufficient – if not purchase more
- The accounts manager and IT manager must make sure there is agreement and funding available

Training

- All new staff should be trained to use UB sw and hw as part of their induction programme
- All staff should be trained if there are any major upgrades
- This will mean that HR must develop a policy and programme for induction and training
- This programme must include coverage of legislation affecting UB
- This should include H&S
- It should also include instruction of the use and misuse of the intranet
- All staff must have an understanding of preservation and protection of data and information

Security and backup

- The IT manager must set up a programme of back ups so that vital details are not lost
- I suggest that this is done on a daily basis to prevent loss of business information and customers
- All staff should be given a password to access areas of the system
- Different staff should be given access to specific areas so that misuse cannot take place
- Firewalls and other external measures should be in place to prevent hackers accessing the system

Tutor feedback

Some aspects have been addressed rather briefly, especially some of the impacts on the organisation, but the content has been attempted sufficiently well to award P5.

You do not mention the use of customer information in your slides; however, you did relate each issue to the holding of customer information by UB.

Summary

- On the previous slides various action points have been listed
- All these should be considered as aspects of the proposed organisational policy
- The legal aspects will govern how staff in UB work and collect and use information
- The ethical issues will concentrate on the manner in which the staff operate internally and externally
- The operational issues will govern how the IT systems are set up, secured and operated
- It is important to have a policy that all staff operate by to ensure that UB does not infringe any guidelines
- All staff must be familiar with the policy through regular training events

The summary was an excellent addition, as was the way you invited and responded to questions; together, they closed the presentation well.

I see no reason why you would not be able to deliver this presentation to the organisation in question once you add the extra slide identified here.

You have achieved P5.

Well done.